PRAISE FOR
The Path of the Hedge Witch

"*The Path of the Hedge Witch* is a delightful book—a rich compendium of lore packed full of insight and practical guidance to form your own path into Hedge Witchcraft, drawing on deep roots and solid experience. Joanna's books are always a treat, and this is a sound and trusted guide to those new to the practice, covering all you need to know to weave your own traditional magic and showing you how to fly over the hedge and far away! Highly recommended."—Danu Forest, author of *Celtic Tree Magic* and *Wild Magic*

"*The Path of the Hedge Witch* is a charming walk down the path of the country witch, blending the practical and the otherworldly with ease and grace. Author Joanna van der Hoeven has written a truly original book on solitary Witchcraft for those who wish to make a deeper connection to nature in their own way."—Deborah Blake, author of *The Eclectic Witch's Book of Shadows* and *Everyday Witchcraft*

"Joanna provides a comprehensive, up-to-date, and personal account of her hedge witch path and practices. In this book, the reader is treated to both thorough research as well as the poetic beauty of our wild world. Whether an advanced practitioner or beginner on the path of Hedge Witchery, this book provides all you need to make hedge riding and simple natural magic a part of your life."—Moss Milne, founder of *Spiral Path: Seasonal, Slow and Spiritual Living*, an online resource

"Joanna has written an enchanting and practical book about natural magic that will appeal to the beginner and advanced practitioner alike. Written in an easy, conversational style, she offers simple everyday practices that can easily be incorporated into everyday life. Above all, she encourages us to listen to our hearts and souls rather than follow complex, established traditions, and she emphasizes the importance of trusting our own experience as we explore the beauty and wisdom of the natural world. An invaluable handbook for the budding hedge witch!"—Mara Freeman, author of *Kindling the Celtic Spirit* and director of the Avalon Mystery School

"Reading this book is like coming home. Joanna van der Hoeven leads us between the worlds, exploring the path of the hedge witch while encouraging us to weave our own relationship with the Mysteries. Practical and poetic, *The Path of the Hedge Witch* opens a portal to the immanent divinity of the natural world, guiding us to learn the art of hedge riding with a magical compendium of ritual, spellcraft, plant allies, and folklore. I am utterly enchanted."—Danielle Blackwood, author of *The Twelve Faces of the Goddess* and *A Lantern in the Dark*

The Path of the
HEDGE WITCH

About the Author

Joanna van der Hoeven has been working in Pagan traditions for nearly thirty years. She is an author, teacher, dancer, blogger, photographer, and videographer. Her love of nature and the land where she lives provides her with constant inspiration. She was born in Quebec, Canada, and now lives near the sea in Suffolk, England.

The Path of the
HEDGE WITCH

Simple Natural Magic and
the Art of Hedge Riding

Joanna van der Hoeven

LLEWELLYN PUBLICATIONS

WOODBURY, MINNESOTA

FIRST EDITION
First Printing, 2022

Cover art by Jessica Roux
Cover design by Cassie Willett
Illustrations by Llewellyn Art Department
Interior design by Rebecca Zins

Llewellyn is a registered trademark of Llewellyn Worldwide Ltd.

Library of Congress Cataloging-In-Publication Data
Pending
ISBN 978-0-7387-7228-8

Llewellyn Publications
A Division of Llewellyn Worldwide Ltd.
2143 Wooddale Drive
Woodbury, MN 55125-2989

www.llewellyn.com
Printed in the United States of America

Thank you to my family, who have always supported me.
I know I'm not the only nut from this family tree.

To my witchy friends: may you always keep the magic alive.

Special thanks to my editors, Elysia Gallo and Rebecca Zins,
for all their help in making this book the best it could be.

CONTENTS

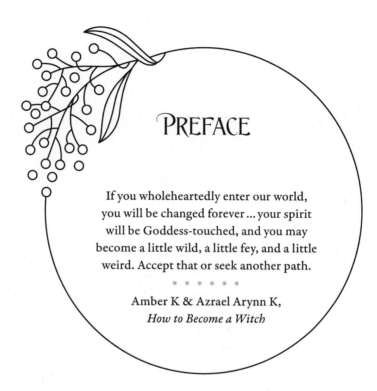

PREFACE

If you wholeheartedly enter our world,
you will be changed forever ... your spirit
will be Goddess-touched, and you may
become a little wild, a little fey, and a little
weird. Accept that or seek another path.

· · · · · ·

Amber K & Azrael Arynn K,
How to Become a Witch

I spent far too many years making other people's opinions my own. My life is my own to live, and while it's important to hear the voices and opinions of others, it's also equally important to have your own, based on your own experience, your own life, your joys and your struggles. Other people's stories are not irrelevant, but they are their stories, not your stories.

Being a hedge witch is about learning to listen to your voice. It is about finding your own inner strength, your own power. It is about connecting to nature. When we find our voice, we also need to speak up with it, if only to sing with the blackbird at dusk. Being a hedge witch is feeling in tune with the cycles of nature, the flows and rhythms of the earth and the sea, of the sky, of the cosmos. It is about the simplicity of honouring the natural world through practical means. It is about understanding the beauty in all things, from the beauty of the sunbeam that works its way across the wall, the dappled sunlight through the leaves of the tree in full summer, the flash of lightning in a thunderstorm, the mysteries of the galaxy whirling in its cosmic round.

Listen to your heart, listen to your soul.
If we can't trust our instincts—if we can't
find the voice of nature—then we
will never find our own.

It is important to do your research, to do your homework. It is important to hear the stories of others, but do not make the mistake that I did: do not make them your own. Their stories are their stories, and your story is your story, and every story will be different, and that is the beauty of Hedge Witchcraft. Each and every practitioner is different. Each and every practitioner sees life through the lens of their own perspective, their own intelligence, their own emotions, and their own power.

If you picked up this book, then you may very well be a hedge witch: one who longs to dance under the moon, sing to the stars, walk between the worlds, honour the times and tides of life and the cycles of the sun, kiss the earth, to feel the power in your belly, find harmony, and discover the enchantment that lies in every single thing. This is your path. No one can walk it for you.

Blessings on your journey.

Joanna van der Hoeven
Imbolc 2021

INTRODUCTION

Be hole, be dust, be dream, be wind
Be night, be dark, be wish, be mind
Now slip, now slide, now move unseen
Above, beneath, betwixt, between.

• • • • • •

Neil Gaiman,
The Graveyard Book

I have been a witch for as long as I can remember. I have always been enchanted by the sound of the wind through the pine trees and the last rays of the setting sun illuminating the sky. I have a special rapport with animals and often have prophetic dreams. I feel the rhythms of nature flowing around me and through me, and I have always honoured the cycles and the seasons, though I may not have always had a name, ritual form, or tradition to describe it fully. It has always been easy for me to connect with the natural world, find solace in the wild places with animals and plants, and walk among the seen and the unseen.

Some might know me from my work as a druid, which has for many years been an outward manifestation of my love for the earth. But inwardly, I also consider myself a hedge witch, dancing under the moon and laughing with the incoming tide. My path of Witchcraft is something that is extremely personal and something that is really just for me. Though I sometimes share ritual with others and am part of several Pagan organisations, my daily path is filled with the magic of Witchcraft and my own Hedge Witchcraft tradition. It is a simple, practical, down-to-earth tradition. It deals largely with the folk of the otherworld, and my life is blessed and enhanced from my worldly and otherworldly experiences. And now I am honoured to share that part of myself with you, alongside all my other works in the realms of Druidry.

The term *hedge witch* can mean so many things to so many people. I love the fact that so many forms of Witchcraft incorporate what works for the individual, and so you may find a witch calling on Christian saints while chanting over herbal potions or using other techniques such as working with the chakras, bushcrafting, spirit journeys, or myriad other forms that all have relevance to the individual. And this is where the stress must be emphasised:

Hedge Witchcraft is for the individual. The relevance is for the person doing the work. Hedge witches do not need to conform to anyone else's ideas of what is and isn't acceptable, what is or isn't right. They have their own morals and ethics, and they think hard and long on these things. They work with the earth and the seasons, the moon and the tides, and they know where they stand in their own ecosystem. They cannot be labelled into one specific tradition that has rules and regulations. They are simply followers of the Old Ways.

As well, since I work so much with the liminal spaces and the otherworld, in my practice hedge riding is the heart of the Craft. It becomes a part of me, of how I live my life each and every day. I walk with one foot in each world, so I see the beauty and gifts that each presents, as well as the challenges. It has greatly informed my practice, and my life has been enriched from these experiences. It is what truly makes me a hedge witch.

This book is about the simple practice and spirituality of the hedge witch. It is not a book on Wicca. Although it is perfectly fine to be a Wiccan hedge witch, I feel that the breadth of that topic would require a whole book in itself, so this book focuses on the old folklore and customs of the country witch, the hedge riding tradition, and the magical arts of the countryfolk.

Hedge Witchcraft is a wonderful path of exploration, and you don't need to narrow your focus to just one specific form or tradition. You will always be learning on the path of Witchcraft. You will always be free to study and learn what *you* want, not what someone tells you that you should do. In this work I call my own path Hedge Witchcraft to denote the practices found within this tradition, but you may find another name for your tradition or use none at all. You can incorporate things that you like from other traditions, as many witches in the past have done and will continue to do in the future. As long as you honour the context in which a tradition or practice evolved and give it all due respect without using it inappropriately, then all should be well. If witches of the past and of today had a motto, it would probably be this: If it works, do it!

This book is intended as an introductory guide to help you find your own path and way of working as a witch. It is a simple path, one that requires few tools or complex rituals, relying on the relationship with nature alongside traditional and folkloric knowledge. It provides guidance for a solitary path, one that calls on your own wits and intelligence, integrity and strength. It is also about the art of hedge riding, of walking between the worlds in your Craft. We work with the Fair Folk (faeries) and other spirits to learn more about this world and the otherworld, and use that information in our daily lives.

Note what you agree with in this work and what you do not agree with, and ask yourself why in both situations. Try out the rituals; experiment. Don't follow or do what appears in this book without thought, and if something doesn't speak to you or you feel that it isn't right for your path, then simply don't do it. Discern for yourself what you feel will be applicable to your path and your life, both from this book and from all other books and teachings you may receive in the Craft. Just because you disagree with something in a book doesn't mean you have to stop reading and put it away. I've learned over the many years I've been practising that it's possible to disagree with an author on one issue and see something that really speaks to my soul in the next chapter of their work. Take what you want, leave the rest, as long as you respect the context in which it derives and belongs.

This book is intended for both beginners and as a good refresher for those who have travelled down the path of the witch for some time. The rites and rituals are guidance and inspiration only, for in this path you must find your own footing that works for you personally. For me, the path of the hedge witch is a personal quest, one that never allows me to become complacent and one that requires me to think for myself. We learn discernment and due diligence, respect and admiration for the wonderful teachings of the Craft. We never stop learning.

I hope that this book inspires you in the Craft and brings your world the wisdom of nature and the enchantment that comes from living a truly magical life. I love the freedom of Hedge Witchcraft. I am at my freest when I'm out in the wilds alone, communing with the nature spirits and the Fair Folk, the gods and goddesses that walk this land. When I am watching a herd of deer running through the wood or I hear the clarion cry of a hawk circling overhead, I know that I am home. This is what has always run through my veins; it is the song that has always been sung deep within my soul. I know that there is magic all around me, and I have always known.

And now I am able to share that enchantment with you.

So may it be.

PART 1

Defining the Terms & Looking at History

*In this section, we take a look at just what
Witchcraft is, the history of Witchcraft,
and what it means to be a hedge witch,
including taking on a solitary practice.*

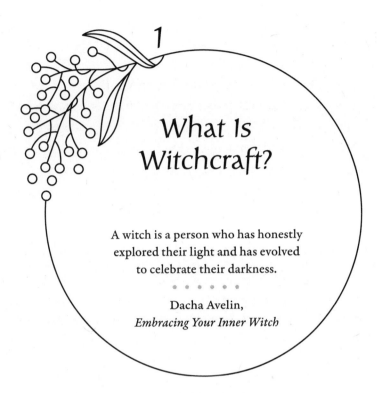

What Is Witchcraft?

A witch is a person who has honestly
explored their light and has evolved
to celebrate their darkness.

• • • • • •

Dacha Avelin,
Embracing Your Inner Witch

Witchcraft is setting the soul free. It is wild. It is singing with the blackbirds at dusk, learning the ways of the land, and living an enchanted existence. It is knowledge and power, the wisdom gained from observation and experience felt deep within the bones of the body and the earth. It is magic, the inner sovereignty gained from being able to shape and change your world.

It is for everyone, regardless of age, gender, social status, race, or circumstance. It is the longing held deep within each heart to truly be as you have always wished to be in the world and then make that happen.

It is learning about your local environment: where the deer hide in the heat of a midsummer day, where the ants are nesting, where the spiders weave their webs, where the owls roost. It is knowing where your drinking water comes from, what plants grow in your area, what the weather patterns are and how they affect everything around you. Witchcraft is learned and felt in the blood that flows through your veins and in the energy patterns flowing through this planet, interacting with the moon and stars and everything else in this universe.

Witchcraft is knowing that there is more to this world than what the eye can see in plain sight. It is the knowledge of the otherworld, where the Fair Folk reside, and when and where the veils are thin, allowing travel between the worlds. It is the courage to travel to these realms, to experience and communicate with other beings, to gain further knowledge and wisdom to bring back to your world. It is working in friendship and good relationship with beings from both worlds, offering respect and amity.

Above all, Witchcraft is about being present each and every day. It is knowing what is going on in the world around you—your own local environment and the world at large. It is watching the buds open on the birch trees in the spring and feeling the sticky leaves unfurl in the sunlight. It is knowing the phases of the moon and where the sun rises and sets each day. It is knowing your own mind and your own moods, emotions, triggers, and strengths. It is knowledge of the self and of others around you.

The Roots of Witchcraft

Witchcraft is a practice that is as old as the hills. It is a skill in the arts of magic, healing, herbcraft, psychology, animal husbandry, and more. It has been practised all over the world by every single civilisation throughout time.

Just as Witchcraft has been celebrated and held in high esteem, in various forms Witchcraft also has been persecuted by many religions and people in positions of power throughout the ages. Today, Western civilisation incorporates a much broader view of the world, and therefore Witchcraft is not nearly as persecuted as it was before, with basic universal human rights having improved as we move towards a global worldview. Yet there are still pockets of hate and misunderstanding, even here in the West, where sometimes it can be dangerous to claim to be a witch or be associated with Witchcraft.

In Britain the Witchcraft Acts of 1562 and 1604 were repealed in 1951. These laws stated that practice of Witchcraft was punishable by death. In 1736 Parliament passed an act repealing the laws against Witchcraft, but it also gave out fines or prison sentences for those who claimed to have magical powers.[1] The old Act was then replaced by the Fraudulent Mediums Act in 1951, and therefore Witchcraft gained most of its freedom once again. In 2008 the Fraudulent Mediums Act was also repealed, and the freedom to practice without worry was finally in place.

The word *witch* has a much debated origin. Some believe it relates to the use of "wit" or in relation to "wise," as in a wisewoman or a wiseman: someone who had skills and knowledge and who could be turned to in times of trouble within the community. In Old English *wicca* was the masculine form, *wicce* the feminine, with *wiccan* being the plural; later, *wicche* was used for both the masculine and the feminine.[2] The Old English word for Witchcraft is *wiccecræft*, from *wicce* (witch) and *cræft* (craft), which is where we derive our modern-day term. There are those who believe that *wicce* means "to bend or shape," as it relates to the word *willow*, a resource often used to create very useful items through bending or shaping. This action could also refer to the bending or shaping of fate, through magical or other means, hence the word *witch* may have its roots (pardon the pun) in *willow*. There are other theories, of course, and all are plausible, and none are proven as fact.

Witchcraft comes in many forms and traditions. It can be seen as an umbrella term that covers a multitude of traditions. As well, it can also be used to differentiate anything that isn't connected to the more modern Wicca. Where I live on the Suffolk Coast there are both Wiccans and followers of British Traditional Witchcraft, a form of Witchcraft rooted in the land and folklore and not belonging to the modern traditions such as Wicca. Another "name" for it is the Nameless Tradition, which I first

---

1 UK Parliament, "Witchcraft."
2 Valiente, *An ABC of Witchcraft*, 343.

discovered through the works of Val Thomas, a witch living in the neighbouring county of Norfolk.[3]

Wicca, a modern form of Witchcraft, is a fast-growing religious tradition stemming from the older traditions of Witchcraft. It was developed in the mid-twentieth century mostly through the works of Gerald Brosseau Gardner and expounded upon by Doreen Valiente, his associate. After the Witchcraft Act in Britain was repealed, Gardner felt it was time to make public all that he knew about the workings of Witchcraft at the time in Britain (despite committing others of his coven to oaths of secrecy, which caused some contention). Gardner claimed he was fearful of the tradition dying out completely.

Gardner worked closely with a friend, Ross Nichols, to research and develop a system of eight festivals through which a Wiccan could celebrate the turning of the seasons. They mined what they knew of occult lore and present-day Witchcraft and filled in the gaps with folklore.[4] Gerald Gardner later became known as the "father of modern Witchcraft," and Ross Nichols founded the Order of Bards, Ovates and Druids, one of the largest Druid organisations known today across the globe. It was Doreen Valiente who put Gardner's work together into a cohesive form and rewrote some of the material with her talent as a poet and a writer. Many would call her the "mother of modern Witchcraft," and I would not disagree in the least. Valiente's contributions are vast; to find out more about her, please do read her biography by Philip Heselton, which is fascinating!

In Britain Witchcraft can be seen as the inheritance of the indigenous magical traditions of these lands alongside other forms of Paganism such as Druidry. Sometimes this form of Witchcraft is known as British Traditional Witchcraft.

It is important to note that Witchcraft and Satanism are two very different things. Most practitioners of Witchcraft do not worship the Christian devil and therefore could not be Satanists. Sadly, even to this day there are

---

3   Thomas, *Of Chalk and Flint.*
4   Carr-Gomm, *The Origin of Wicca and Druidry.*

many who confuse Witchcraft with Satanism and use Satanism to denote anything outside of their accepted worldview that they wish to impose upon others or profit from. Interestingly, Romany forest dwellers in Britain (often associated with Witchcraft and previously known as "Gypsies") were said to have honoured a Pagan god called "Duvel": Could this have been where the association of Witchcraft and the devil first originated?[5] The devil and Satanism always make for a thrilling story. Hollywood and horror films have done much to colour people's view of what Witchcraft is and made a bundle of cash in the process of creating this fiction.

Witchcraft is often seen as specific traditions within the broader umbrella term of Paganism. The term *Pagan* derives from the Latin word *paganus*, which originally was a Roman term for someone who lived in a rural setting, versus the city dweller, or *cives* (from which we get *civilisation*). Much of Paganism is rooted in the lore and craft of the countryside, of working with the tides of nature and allowing nature to guide one in daily life. In modern Paganism we find many traditions that honour nature in myriad forms, such as Wicca and Witchcraft, but also Druidry, Heathenry, and more, with the simple term *Paganism* to define one's path if one wants to avoid a label.

Witchcraft is something that can be practised by all. It can be found deep in the heart of a city or out in the wild and windy moors. Wherever we are in the world, we are always surrounded by nature, whether that is the sunlight or moonlight, the wind, clouds, and rain. Rivers flow past cities, and the earth still hums beneath the concrete. Parks are often pockets of green magic where the enchantment flows on a smaller scale. A blade of grass that grows up from a sidewalk crack, the gorgeous London plane tree (a hybrid of the American sycamore and the English Oriental plane), the Norway maple in New York City, the pigeon nesting on the roof of your building: all these are parts of nature that you can interact with.

In this work, the Witchcraft presented here is a blend of many things: my own personal knowledge and skill, inborn talents, teachings received,

---

5 Valiente, *An ABC of Witchcraft*, 86.

in-depth research, and practical application that I have gained over my thirty years in the tradition. It is a blend of many influences, suited for the solitary seeker who works and walks between the worlds. I will provide the well-known information, concepts, and correspondences, but I will also point out that these may not be applicable to you in your particular area. Hedge Witchcraft is very much a local tradition, so things may change dependent upon your situation. Wherever you are, I hope that the journey will be a magical one and that we can bring back the enchantment so needed in our modern-day world.

Blessings in your work!

*S*he walks out into the moonlit back garden, the owls hooting in the trees on the hillside. Everything is covered in silver light, ethereal and magical. She stands in the centre of the garden and raises her hands towards the moon, drinking in its energy and light and also that of the dark shadows cast around her. She spins around and around, filling her soul with the wonder and magic of the night. She stops, dizzy, and then begins to spin her body the other way, unwinding the energy that she has raised within her. She comes to a standstill; the world tilts this way and that before it settles before her. "It's all perspective," a voice whispers in her mind. She laughs aloud her joy and falls down onto the soft grass, placing her hands upon the earth. They shine silvery in the moonlight, and she follows the energy down, down, into the ground. She can feel the energy of the season's tide, the moving and flowing, the waxing and waning. She then lies back upon the ground and looks up into the starry expanse of the heavens. She knows who she is and where her place is in this world, and she is free.

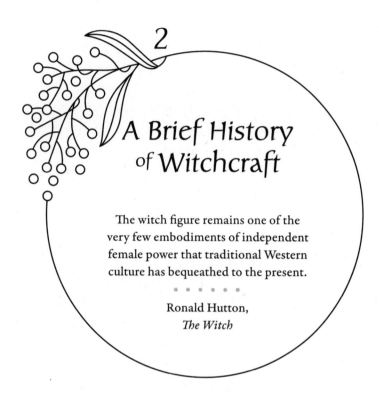

2

A Brief History of Witchcraft

The witch figure remains one of the very few embodiments of independent female power that traditional Western culture has bequeathed to the present.

. . . . . .

Ronald Hutton,
The Witch

Witchcraft has probably been around as long as human consciousness has, in some form or other. It can take many forms, from a shamanic and animistic practice to one that uses very modern formal and complex rites, rituals, and correspondences. At the heart of Witchcraft is the ability to create change in the world, to take control of aspects of our lives and the natural world around us in order to bring about the desired outcome.

Witchcraft in the Ancient World

It is difficult to separate Witchcraft from religious or spiritual traditions found in the history of ancient humanity. As we simply do not know what they believed, we can only make assumptions based on what we find through archaeology and anthropology. There are tantalising examples of cave art from our Stone Age ancestors, where we see human beings with animal qualities performing rituals of a sort. We assume that the cave paintings and statuary/figurines represent god/goddess images or their priests/priestesses; however, that is still an assumption. The rites and rituals that may have accompanied these items would have elements of what we know today as Witchcraft and perhaps evolved from them. At the very least, we can deduce from the artwork that they *had* religious or spiritual traditions, but what exactly these were is anyone's guess.

It's yet another assumption, but one many are happy to make, that throughout history there have been those who have been seen as different, as set apart from the normal lives and routines of others, whether it be in a tribe or a community. These people may have had highly developed sensitivities and were able to predict the weather, for example (I personally always know when the pressure is changing from a high to a low front; I can feel it in my head and my ears pop). They may have had a near-death experience that granted them the ability to deal with death and the dying. They may have known where certain herbs grew that could heal specific wounds. Notice that I say "may" in each of these sentences because we just don't really know for sure, and it would be irresponsible for me to say otherwise.

Witchcraft in the Middle Ages

We can get a somewhat clearer (though still heavily biased) picture when it comes to actual recorded history, not only of what was perceived to be Witchcraft, but of the patriarchal system that totally feared losing its power and authority. In the Middle Ages, when men, women, and sometimes even children were persecuted for Witchcraft, it seems very unlikely that the majority were actual practitioners of the art. When we look at the reasons stated for their persecution, we see the seedy underbelly of humanity's unkindness and greed. Neighbour who hated neighbour could raise an allegation without evidence. Corrupt churchmen could do the same in order to gain the lands and profit from those that were hanged or burnt at the stake (witches here hanged in England and New England and burned in Scotland and Europe). Many were condemned as heretics, not witches. But what was recorded from these witch trials passed into the folk memory, and certain ideas came about concerning Witchcraft. Some may have truth; some may be completely the deranged and perverted dreams of the men who seemed to enjoy torturing their captives and extorting a false confession. At any rate, the inflammatory persecution and hysteria had begun.

In these times it was alleged that Witchcraft consisted of making deals with the devil and consorting with the devil in various ways. The devil could influence you to do or say things that you would not do otherwise. Sabbaths, the witches' gatherings, were said to consist of singing, dancing, and drinking (sounds like fun to me). In the very strict growing Puritan faith, all of these were taboo in varying degrees. One could also be possessed by a witch, who could fly out of her body and take over the body of another person.

The *Malleus Maleficarum,* or *Hammer of the Witches*, written by Heinrich Kramer and Jacob Sprenger in 1486, was the handbook used for witch hunters. Section I argues that because the devil exists and has the power to do astounding things, witches exist to help, if done through the aid of the devil and with the permission of God (which is odd, to say the least). The devil's power is greatest where human sexuality is concerned, for it was believed that women were more sexual than men. Loose women had sex with the devil, thus paving their way to become witches. The *Malleus* states that all Witchcraft comes from carnal lust, which is "insatiable in women."

In section II of the *Malleus Maleficarum*, the authors turn to matters of practice by discussing actual cases. This section first discusses the powers of witches and then goes into recruitment strategies. It is mostly witches as opposed to the devil who do the recruiting by making something go wrong in the life of a respectable matron that makes her consult the knowledge of a witch or by introducing young maidens to tempting young devils. This section also details how witches cast spells and the remedies that can be taken to prevent Witchcraft or help those that have been affected by it (usually bought from those who are persecuting Witchcraft). Sometimes, if one didn't buy an anti-witch charm from the witch hunter, they would be persecuted as a witch themselves. Go figure.

Section III is the legal part of the *Malleus* that describes how to prose-cute a witch. The arguments are clearly defined for the lay magistrates pros-ecuting witches. It offers a step-by-step guide to the conduct of a witch trial, from the method of initiating the process and assembling accusations to the interrogation of witnesses and the formal charging of the accused. Women who did not cry during their trial were automatically believed to be witches. Three hundred years on, books of a similar vein were still being written to find and prosecute witches. It is my personal opinion (and one also shared by many today) that the material contained in these books says a lot more about the authors than they do about Witchcraft and those who were persecuted.

Later in the seventeenth century, we see King James I (IV Scotland) was a staunch believer in Witchcraft, as was his mother Queen Elizabeth I (she famously even retained an astrologer, Dr. John Dee, as part of her retinue and as her advisor). James I was so fearful of Witchcraft that he published a treatise, *Daemonologie,* to support the witch hunts.[6] As well, during his reign the wording in the Bible was changed to read "Thou shalt not suffer a *witch* to live" where before it stated "Thou shalt not suffer a *poisoner* to live."[7] In the seventeenth century, Witchcraft was real and threatening (at least to the establishment), and if you did not believe, you could be labelled a heretic or a witch yourself.

Witchcraft in the New World

In the Salem witch trials held from 1692–1693 in New England, the incredible concept of *spectral evidence* was used in court, which consisted of the testimony of an afflicted person who could see the shape of the per-son who was allegedly afflicting them. Yes, really. The court contended that

6   Goodare, "A Royal Obsession with Black Magic."
7   Brigham Young University, "The Life and Legacy of the King James Bible."

permission was necessary by the witch for the devil to assume the witch's shape in order to influence others to their ways. Increase Mather, the father of the infamous Cotton Mather, was one of many who doubted such evidence could be upheld at court, stating that spectral evidence was not merely enough on its own to convict one of Witchcraft. He still defended the judges and magistrates, however, so he was skilled at sitting on both sides of the fence. He published a book entitled *Cases of Conscience*, which spoke out against the shaky testimony and absence of hard evidence, while still defending the status quo.

Cotton Mather was influential in upholding spectral evidence to begin an investigation into Witchcraft and bring someone to trial. All in all, both Increase and Cotton Mather to different degrees fanned the flames of persecution in the New World.

Punishment for Witchcraft varied according to the country in which one was persecuted. As previously stated, in Europe and Scotland, witches were burned. In England and America, witches were hanged. Various methods of torture were used, such as the rack and pressing, which involved laying stones on the chest of the accused, gradually increasing the weight until they either confessed, named other witches, or died. For the Salem witch trials, the court mistakenly believed that pressing was still legal, when in fact it had been abolished in England twenty years earlier.

The Salem witch trials were held just after a tumultuous time in New England. Salem, Massachusetts, is in the Eastern seaboard region of the United States. It was full of natural resources and under attack from both the French and their Native American allies time and again. The newly appointed governor for Massachusetts was William Phips, and one of his first duties was to create a Special Court of Oyer and Terminer to handle the large numbers of people in Salem's jails.

Salem village was torn apart by land disputes, as well as by those who were against the appointment of Samuel Parris as their first ordained minister. Parris was to receive the deed to his parsonage (which was previously voted against by the parishioners) as part of the lengthy and detailed package that took over five months to draft and agree upon, and which afterwards still caused problems in the community.[8] Eventually they settled for Parris, having had three previous ministers already in a short space of time.

Children of varying ages, from four to twelve years of age, were the accusers in the trials. One of the first to be accused was Tituba, a slave girl/woman, her background often believed to be Caribbean. Sarah Good was another of the initially accused, a poor woman who was known to beg for food and shelter from her neighbours. Sarah Osborne, who had married her indentured servant, was another among the early accused. They fit the description of the usual suspects as they did not conform or fit into Puritan society. Over 150 people were arrested and imprisoned, and the court convicted twenty-nine, nineteen of whom were executed.

When the trials were later found to be false and full of lies, folly, and superstition, families of those executed later received compensation. Sadly, those who had been excommunicated had been buried together in a shallow, unmarked grave. However, oral history claims that the families retrieved the bodies and buried them in unmarked graves upon their personal properties. Those that had been named but had fled returned to find their homes plundered and had to fight for compensation.

Reverand John Hale, who was present at many of the Salem proceedings, wrote a book entitled *A Modest Enquiry into the Nature of Witchcraft* in 1697. In it he expressed remorse and regret at what had taken place, stating, "Such was the darkness of the day, the tortures and lamentations of the afflicted ... that we walked in the clouds and could not see our way."[9]

The End of Legal Persecution

In 1736 King George I passed a Witchcraft Act, which stated that Witchcraft wasn't real, so people should stop being persecuted as witches. However, those who *pretended* to have supernatural powers could still be

---

8 Baker, "Samuel Parris: Minister at Salem Village."
9 Wilson, *The Salem Witch Trials*, 51.

punished. He did not believe that there were real witches, only people pretending to be witches and have the powers of Witchcraft. In 1951 the Witchcraft Act was fully repealed in Britain and replaced with the Fraudulent Mediums Act, which was repealed in 2008.[10]

Witchcraft in the Nineteenth and Twentieth Centuries

In the nineteenth century there was a revival of magic, religion, and the occult supported by the works of Sir James Frazer in *The Golden Bough: A Study in Magic and Religion*. Paintings by romantic artists as well as the popularity of the Celtic Twilight movement helped turn people's minds from the industrial to the pastoral and the myths and mysteries that lay in the land. At the turn of the twentieth century, famous anthropologist and suffragette Margaret Alice Murray became popular, though in these last twenty years her works have been the subject of much controversy. She is known to have advanced the idea that Witchcraft is the Old Religion, and that it stemmed from a matriarchal culture. This idea had already been put forward by Charles Godfrey Leland, who wrote about and practised Witchcraft. In 1888 he claimed to be initiated into *La Vecchia Religione* (The Old Religion) in Italy and subsequently wrote a book called *Aradia, or the Gospel of the Witches*. Whether Leland's claims are true or false we will probably never know, but Murray expounded on this idea to create the concept that those persecuted of Witchcraft in the Middle Ages were really part of an ancient goddess/fertility religion still being practised. Again, sadly, there is no evidence to prove this interesting theory and quite a bit to prove to the contrary.

When the Witchcraft Act was repealed, people started to come out of the broom closet. Gerald Brosseau Gardner was one of the first. As mentioned earlier, Gardner was the one who came up with the word *Wica* to denote his spiritual path. Why it was spelt in this fashion is unclear, for we have written evidence of the word *wiccan* in the Laws of King Alfred circa

10   UK Parliament, "Witchcraft."

890 CE, and also in Aldhelm's *Glossary* in 1100 CE.[11] I guess Gardner just preferred it that way, or maybe he used it to denote that his tradition was different from the former *wicces*.

Naturism was a big fashion in the 1920s and '30s, and Gardner was a naturist (hence the *skyclad*—being naked—part of his particular tradition of Witchcraft). There was even a naturist camp that opened up near his home in England. He became involved in the Rosicrucian Theatre and later came across Masonic (Fellowship of Crotona) practices and the work of Margaret Murray, which he incorporated into his ideas for this spiritual path. Gardner came up with beautiful poetry for his tradition, which was also a contentious point for one of Gardner's high priestesses, the aforementioned Doreen Valiente (who believed, like many others have since, that it had been taken directly from the infamous Aleister Crowley's work[12]). Like Leland, Gardner claimed to have learned his Witchcraft from an older woman who was part of a hereditary or initiatory tradition. Gardner created the Witchcraft that he was seeking, and Valiente wrote it down eloquently and made sense of it all.[13] Valiente herself was a highly intelligent, talented woman and witch, and also a wonderful poet; her work is still being used by many witches to this very day.

Others expounded upon the work of Gardner and Valiente, including the famous/infamous Alex Sanders, self-proclaimed "King of the Witches." Sanders took the work of others and proclaimed it as his own in many instances (a failing that is still repeated across many traditions today, but which was particularly rife back then), calling it Alexandrian. However, he did leave a legacy of teaching within the tradition, which was something Gardner did not do in his own coven (a coven is a group of witches/Wiccans working together). His wife, Maxine, continues to teach and lecture today, and she has some fabulous stories to tell.

---

11   Valiente, *An ABC of Witchcraft*, 343.
12   Crowley was dubbed "the wickedest man on earth" due to his sexual licentiousness, drug addiction, and anti-Victorian attitudes at the time.
13   Heselton, *Doreen Valiente: Witch*.

In 1972 Witchcraft was recognised legally in America as a religion and was tax-exempt by the IRS, so "churches" of Wicca sprang up. The priests and priestesses had the same rights as any ordained clergy. Feminist branches of Wicca and Witchcraft began to emerge and further the cause of feminism and the empowerment of women, mainly through the work of author and activist Starhawk and the Reclaiming organisation that she helped found. In the late eighties, eclectic Wicca and Witchcraft became popular through the works of Scott Cunningham, who popularised a solo path for those in the tradition, where before only information on group/coven working was available. In 1990 British author Rae Beth coined the term *hedge witch* to denote one on a solitary path of Witchcraft, and since then it has come to mean many different things.

Witchcraft and Wicca have seen some difficult times in their evolution. Both have, to some extent, suffered and still suffer in some parts of the world from persecution. Media portrayals of both can be very wrong or misleading. Both Wicca and Witchcraft have also suffered from lies and deception in their various stages. Gerald Gardner claimed to have written and devised much of the rites and rituals in his then–newly branded Wica (now called Wicca), but they were found out to be a collection of works from other previously published sources. Sanders revelled in the cult of celebrity that he created around himself, rather than focusing on the spiritual path itself. As stated earlier, it appears Gardner hired Crowley to write the rituals and lore for his new tradition, for which he either took credit himself or accredited it to ancient lore and teaching he had received.[14]

The traditions in the beginnings of the modern-day era seemed to be rife with deception, including claims of authenticity of such matters like lineage, initiation, and so on. Yet these could all be products of a culture that still very much depended upon concepts such as ancient authenticity rather than validity. Our Victorian predecessors did it all the time in many aspects of life. As well, it was still very much a patriarchal and hierarchical

14 Farrar et al., *The Inner Mysteries*, 31.

culture and society, where a dependence upon authority seemed to be more commonplace. Much emphasis was placed on coven working, initiation, levels of hierarchy, and secrecy in the early days of the 1950s through to the 1980s, influenced by the secret societies of the past and present. Now we see a lessening of the need to make such claims as the traditions gain their own footing on their own merits.

Witchcraft in the Twenty-First Century

Witchcraft has progressed from its early reinventing in the modern era. The term *Progressive Witchcraft* had come about at the turn of the millennium in an attempt to drop the hard edges of labels that can be too restrictive for some. It speaks out against hierarchical authority and the dogma that has been created by some traditions. Concepts such as initiation by another member of a coven as the only route to validity and true acceptance is falling by the wayside as new generations of coven members adopt different ways. Solitary practitioners have found merit in walking their own path, initiated by the gods or the natural world around them either in solo ritual or at various points with others in their own lives. It is a doing away with some of the hierarchic systems that keep all the power within the roles of high priest and high priestess. More and more covens are now totally democratic, allowing each person to take on different roles for a set amount of time, and high priest/priestess simply denotes the person who is leading at that particular time. There are many groups now that work within a system of shared responsibility rather than strict hierarchy. There might still be leaders in the community, but "authority figures" seem to be falling by the wayside as people realise that the cult of celebrity is a hollow thing.

More people are gaining respect and notice within the Pagan community as a whole based upon the work that they *do* rather than what they *say* about themselves. There is less of an ego-driven need behind the work and rather a growing trend towards service to the community or the earth itself as the guiding force behind it all.

We see that Witchcraft is still progressing and always will: for a craft, religious, or spiritual tradition that doesn't evolve is dry and dead. It must meet the needs of the time and grow alongside those who follow its tenets. The modern Witchcraft revival may have had some dubious claims made by the original trailblazers desperate to authenticate and therefore validate their paths, but we have now outgrown that need as we are less dependent upon authority and as we rally against patriarchy more and more, with equality at the heart of many matters in today's society. We know that Witchcraft works in all its various forms. We can find a path that is suited to our needs, to our society. If we choose to do so on our own, we might even call ourselves solitaries or even hedge witches.

But what is a hedge witch?

*S*he sighs and closes the book softly, the soft hush of the library all around her. There is so much to learn, so much history. And yet it is important, she reminds herself, to know where we have come from so that we may have an idea as to where we are going in the future. She feels the roots of the past spreading throughout her soul, guiding her to what she feels is right for her today. She looks back to the shelves, and the whispers of the past beckon her further into what she is now and what she could become.

3

The
Solitary Witch
and the Hedge Witch

There are three things which many
modern people appear to fear above
anything else. These are stillness, silence
and solitude, yet these are the very things
which give a witch her or his power.

· · · · · ·

Marian Green,
Natural Witchcraft

The hedge witch is a deliciously enigmatic figure who conjures the image of a person living on the edge of a village, brewing potions from the herbs they have gathered in the wilds and chanting magical spells over it as they stir the cauldron, or cooking pot. Cats wander underfoot or sleep in nooks and niches around the home. It is a cosy, comfortable, simple space, filled with interesting items that have both magical and mundane uses. The smell of herbs and wood smoke lingers in the air, and the abode is both welcoming and mysterious at the same time. They are known to sing to the moon, talk with the birds, predict the weather, and have charms for every known ailment. They often consult the faeries and nature spirits, and they can walk between the worlds. They are the wise folk, the cunning people, figures from out of myth and folklore.

All of these ideas may indeed be true of a hedge witch today. I, for one, do actually live on the edge of a village and collect herbs from my meanderings on the heath and in the forest or just down the lane. I have two cats and a fireplace where I scry (a form of divination) in the flames on cold winter nights. I have herbs drying in my home, but they are in the airing cupboard, as that is the best place I have found for the task! I have several cauldrons, but I cook with stainless steel pans. I do perform magical spells and sing to the moon. I listen to what the blackbirds, starlings, and hawks have to say on any given day, interpreting their calls and chatter after years of listening to them all around me. I have a pharmacy of herbs in an old Victorian cupboard to treat ailments of all kinds. I have met with the Fair Folk (faeries) and talked with spirits of the land all around me. I walk between the worlds.

I also write on a laptop and watch television. I have taught and performed belly dance for over a decade and have my own YouTube channel. I live a fairly "normal" life, at least in my eyes, though others might think what I do is odd or, at the very least, different from most. I do enjoy the eclectic, the unusual, but I also enjoy the simple things, like going to the pub with friends and having a good pint of beer or glass of wine. My home is a 1980s build of red brick with a large garden situated on a quiet cul-de-sac. I used to live on the outskirts of a town but had the opportunity to move back to the country years ago and jumped at the chance. My life is a mix of modern living and discovering old lore, incorporating both into the everyday routine. I honour Pagan gods and goddesses, the ancestors, and more. I live a magical and mundane life at the same time, seeing no division between the two. I work mostly alone in my Craft but sometimes have friends over for the holidays or gather together with one or two for a full moon ritual. Over the years I have re-enchanted my life to reflect who I really am and what I really want to do in the world. My life as a hedge witch reflects that each and every day.

Let's now take a closer look at Hedge Witchcraft: solitary work, hedge riding, and the tradition being one of simplicity.

The Roots of Hedge Witchcraft: Going Solo

Hedge Witchcraft may be seen today as a solitary pursuit, crafting one's life in a magical way that reflects the practitioner's talents and abilities. It also denotes someone who is knowledgeable in the country ways of knowing weather patterns, herbalism, animal husbandry, and more.

> *When author Rae Beth coined the term* hedge witch *in her book* Hedge Witch: A Guide to Solitary Witchcraft *(1992), she took the term* hedge *from the previous label of "hedge priest," one who preached from the hedgerow and had no physical place for a congregation.*

During the Reformation, Calvinist priests held open-air services out of authorities' reach. This was a renegade solitary priest who didn't follow the rules. This still appeals to many today, myself included.

A hedge witch is a bit of an anarchist. They usually prefer to work alone, and they work in their Craft daily, honing their skills and always learning more. They may think differently from those around them: they may see spirits and talk with the ancestors, they may talk to plants or animals, and they certainly walk their talk. They take full responsibility for everything that they do, and they choose carefully. They revere the natural world around them, but they may not necessarily view their path as a religion, instead seeing it as a spiritual practice of working with the land spirits, the fae, the ancestors, and the otherworld.

For the hedge witch, the path may be simply one of life's work, a way of life that honours the cycles of nature without needing the label of religion or spirituality attached. Then again, a hedge witch may honour the gods and goddesses as they please. If you are going to follow a religious bent in your practice, then the Goddess and God will be at the heart of your tradition. Being a hedge witch is for those wishing to honour the world around them in simple everyday rituals and practices, living a life that incorporates the spiritual and the mundane and that is practical, efficient, and works for them.

Solitary Witchcraft

Solitary Witchcraft is just that: Witchcraft that is practised solo. This doesn't mean that solitary witches don't have contact with others or become hermits. It simply means that they practice their Craft on their own. This might be because there are no other witches in the area or they simply prefer to practice the Craft alone. My own personal practice is a solitary one for the most part, but I sometimes do get together for a full moon ritual or a sabbat with friends. I have worked in groups and covens before, but my introverted and solitary feline nature is better suited to solitary practice. Committing oneself to a group or coven doesn't always appeal, as there may be a preference for the freedom of a personal schedule and ritual design. And if one doesn't want to go out and interact with others on a set date, one doesn't have to.

The solitary witch needs discipline. This can sometimes be seen as a four-letter word in modern Paganism, but it's true. Without anyone there to push you or ensure that you keep to your commitment to do a ritual at every full moon and sabbat, you might let your practice slide. Sometimes we just don't feel like doing a ritual at all, and more often than not, those are the precise times when we need to do ritual the most. Ritual is a great reminder of the connection we have to the natural world and to the Goddess and God. In lives that are super busy, where we are constantly running from one thing to another, we often feel we don't have the time or energy for anything other than flopping on the couch after dinner. And so we miss one ritual, and then we stop meditating, and then we miss half a year's worth of work, and then before you know it we're hanging up our pentacle or just reading about Witchcraft instead of practising and experiencing it. It's called a practice for a reason: you have to keep at the Craft and do the work, especially as a solitary, because no one is going to do it for you.

Books are the main teacher for the solitary practitioner. You have the choice to read as much and as varied information as is available to you. It's wonderful. But it can also be confusing, as you will come across some works that don't speak to you or authors that contradict each other. You will have to learn discernment and find out what is right and wrong for your own practice. You will have to research things that are contradictory and come to your own conclusion. If you're lucky, you may have friends who can recommend certain reading. There are plenty of sites where you can find reviews of books as well, but remember that these are only opinions, and yours may differ. Some older books on Witchcraft are a bit outdated now, and some stand the test of time. Those listed in the bibliography of this book are, for this writer, those that have staying power and are written authentically from those who have done the work and who have influenced my own work. Different authors may appeal to you based on their writing styles as well: some people like a direct approach, while others prefer beautiful prose that sparks the imagination. I like both, for different reasons.

As a solitary, you have many choices to make: how you practice, what tools you use, what you wear (or don't wear), what deities you follow; all these and more are choices that you have to make. Some people don't like having to make that many decisions, especially when first starting out on a path. It's easier to follow a guided and established tradition rather than create your own. But the benefit of creating your own path is that it is 100 percent suited to you and no one else. Working as a solitary can be immensely freeing and also immensely challenging. I follow a very simple and solitary form of Witchcraft, so I use the term *witch* or, more specifically, *hedge witch*. Hedge witches have long been connected to the solitary path, so many people find the terms interchangeable.

Pros and Cons of Solitary Work

To recap: when working as a solitary practitioner, you get to decide when, where, and how you practice. You are beholden to no one else's schedule; you can create your own. You can learn from any source that you wish and incorporate what you have learned into your tradition however you see fit. Some people work better on their own and find that the work they do is much deeper in solitary work than in group working. Solitaries can also attend public rituals should they so wish, where they can meet others in the community but without having the restrictions of a particular path set on their learning. There are many online forums and pages where you can talk to others about their paths and learn what they do.

Working as a solitary can sometimes be a little lonely, however, especially if you don't have someone around to physically talk to about your work and your beliefs. Online is all well and good, but face-to-face interaction is a wonderful thing. Not having a dedicated structure for the practice can also hinder the solitary's path; one has to be very disciplined in order to maintain studies and practice, otherwise it can become more of a hobby than a spiritual practice. Some people who believe coven practice is the only way forward may look down on solitaries and disregard the work that they have put into their practice. (Never mind; that's their problem, not yours.) Your study will be entirely self-directed, and so you will realise that no witch, coven, or solitary ever stops learning. However, there is a deeper aspect to working as a hedge witch that not all solitary witches use in their tradition.

What Is the Difference Between a Solitary Witch and a Hedge Witch?

There is more to Hedge Witchcraft than simply working the Craft alone, imbued with local knowledge of the natural world around you, of the green and growing things, of the cycles of the seasons. While many simply see Hedge Witchcraft as the path of a solitary witch, there are others who go deeper into the tradition, discovering the liminal nature of the work.

In her work *The Green Hedge Witch*, author Rae Beth states:

> Hedge Witchcraft works upon and with relationships between humanity and the land, and between this tangible Earth and the elven (fairy) realms. That is its domain. It is this work, private and (usually nowadays) entirely unacknowledged by human society, that

makes Hedge Witchcraft such a profound practice. Traditionally, we hedge witches have aimed to bring balance between what is "beyond the hedge," the realm of wild nature spirits, elves and all creatures, and what is "within the hedge," the human community.[15]

Held deep within the tradition is the art of hedge riding, of walking between the worlds, of being able to find the liminal places and traverse the paths that lead to deeper wisdom and knowledge. This is what separates Solitary Witchcraft from Hedge Witchcraft. The boundaries between this world and the otherworld are manifold; you only have to know where to look. Hedges, as liminal places demarcating one place from another, from the homestead to the wilderness, are wonderful places to use for just such an endeavour. To go through the hedge is to travel into another world, to follow the heart into the wilds and receive information to bring back into this world. It is stepping outside of the known and into the unknown. Though this is not unfamiliar to many coven-based practices, and some covens may indeed work similarly with the liminal, Hedge Witchcraft is usually seen as a solitary practice, working with the forces of the natural world around you, both the seen and the unseen.

Hedge Riding

Hedge riding goes back hundreds of years. We get the term *hedge riding* from a German word, *hagazissa*, which means "hedge sitter."[16] This is also where we get our modern English word *hag*, which many will find familiar in relation to Witchcraft as it is often portrayed in secular culture. This is one who straddles the boundaries of this world and the next, of time and space, the known and the unknown, the civilised and the wild. They could ride that boundary line into the otherworld to talk with spirits and the fey folk and bring healing and other information back to their community. Working with hedges and trees has long been a part of magical traditions the world over. Druidry is a Pagan tradition deeply connected to trees, as

---

15 Beth, *The Green Hedge Witch*, 16.
16 Beth, *The Green Hedge Witch*, 19.

the word *druid* means "wisdom of the oak."[17] The hedge witch operates in much the same function but perhaps in a less formal way, not so much in the role of priest as the druids of old were, but in the cunning folk who cared in other ways for the community.

> *The art of hedge riding can still be*
> *seen today in the traditional portrait*
> *of a witch riding her broom.*

The broom is the magical tree that takes her to other worlds, and in this work we will learn how the use of trees, staffs, wands, brooms, and more relates back to this concept. The hedge is a symbol of the world tree, the axis mundi, that so many religious and spiritual traditions the world over use in their cosmology. Through this world tree we find the roads leading to the faery realms, the realms of the ancestors, and the realms of the gods.

The shamanic nature of hedge riding appeals to many within the tradition who are aware of the hedge-riding nature of this path. It is learning through journeys in the mind and spirit, as well as in the physical, to access information that can be useful in everyday life. It also re-enchants our world, allowing us to see the beauty that lies all around us, the magical and the wonderful, the awe-inspiring moments that transcend "normal" mundane life. It can be compared to the Northern or Norse tradition of seidr, an ancient trance-based oracular tradition that often uses communication with various beings while leaving your physical body and being between the worlds in an astral form.[18] While seidr in the *Saga of Erik the Red* (the main source of seidr in the lore) is described as a working that involves a group of people sending the practitioner into a trance,[19] hedge riding is a more solitary affair, though it may be used to benefit the com-

17 Carr-Gomm, "Druid Wisdom."
18 Saille, *Hedge Riding*, 3.
19 Paxson, "The Return of the Völva."

munity at large and not just the practitioner. It can be viewed as a form of astral travel, where the consciousness of the hedge witch travels to the otherworld, but it can also be done on the physical as well, where we can use the real-life hedge or other liminal markers to move beyond this realm and into another, with all due precaution and skill. In either aspect, an altered form of consciousness helps us in the work.

With this information gained or gleaned from the otherworld, we can then put it to good use in this world. We might indeed brew up a potion or have a new recipe for a healing tea or tincture. We might be able to locate that lost item now that we've had a little otherworldly guidance. We might be able to find out why we are always repeating the same mistakes or what our local patch of land needs from us in order to be healthy and whole. The uses for hedge riding are limitless. That is not to say it is a whim that we travel between the worlds, for this is indeed serious work, and we are committed to doing it with all honour and integrity.

When crossing the boundaries while hedge riding, we will often get glimpses into the otherworld or even spend time there learning all that we can from beings who are both like us and not like us. I speak of the Fair Folk, otherwise known as faeries, those creatures of the otherworld who are so much a part of Witchcraft here in the British Isles. It was long thought that a witch derived her powers from the faeries, and it is why it is so important in hedge riding that we establish a good relationship with these folk.

A Simple Tradition

As I've hinted at so far in this book, Hedge Witchcraft is also a simple path, a tradition that is both practical and spiritual. There is no need for flashy ritual tools, ceremonial robes, grand titles, and weighty magical tomes. While all these things might appeal to some, for the hedge witch it is about the practicality of the work. It is no less spiritual, inspirational, or magical for its simplicity. It is honest and works very much with a no-frills attitude.

The tools are what you have to hand and most often are what you use in your everyday life. What you choose to wear depends on the situation: if you are traipsing around the countryside in the heat of summer or walking across the moorland in the dead of winter, you will be wearing the appropriate clothing. Most of your work will, in fact, take place outdoors, in the light of the sun or moon or in the betwixt and between hours of twilight. Your spell ingredients are often what you also use for cooking, and your cleaning products are natural ones that you have made yourself. You know the names of the plants that grow in your area, and you have a relationship with them and the wildlife that surround you.

You do not command the elements in showy rituals, calling and dismissing them like wayward children. You have a deep respect and ever-growing relationship with the Fair Folk and other beings you meet in your otherworld journeys, who help you bring knowledge and understanding to your own practice. You treat others as you wish to be treated, whether they are of this world or the otherworld.

Hedge Witchcraft is a very natural spiritual path that uses the energies of the natural world to help create a more beneficial state for all. It is based in reciprocity, for what we take we also give back. We live in the modern world and enjoy its modern conveniences such as healthcare, antibiotics and vaccines, indoor plumbing and heating, electricity, and so on. But we also have great pleasure and gratitude for the gentle spring breeze, the frogs singing in the pond at twilight, the feeling of moonlight on our skin, the cry of the fox, or the gentle caress of a lover's lips. We know what really matters to us, and we try to take nothing for granted. We know that there is more to this world than meets the eye, and we are willing to explore that armed with our knowledge and wits, our courage and our fortitude.

*S*he hears a siren as an ambulance whizzes past her downtown apartment block. She says a quick prayer for the person it is called for, as well as for the drivers and the hospital staff. She takes a deep breath and returns to the here and now. Her one-bedroom home is one filled with enticing and enchanting items, reflecting her own personal Hedge Witchcraft tradition. She honours her place of sanctuary and then turns to her circle of house-plants, her own little hedge here in the heart of the city. She knows them each intimately, and they lend their aid to her work. As she steps into the circle of plants, she knows that she is crossing the boundary between worlds, and the magic begins...

PART 2

Learning Through Nature

*In this section, we will explore how the
world around us informs us in our Craft.*

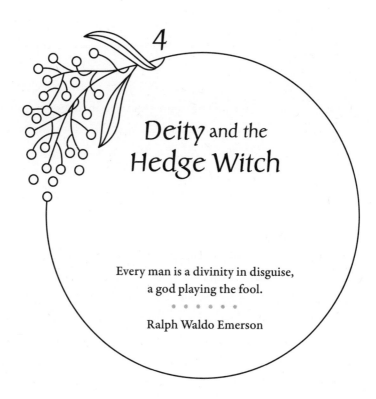

Deity *and the* Hedge Witch

4

Every man is a divinity in disguise,
a god playing the fool.

· · · · · ·

Ralph Waldo Emerson

Many witches work with deity in the form of a twin or dual deity concept of the Goddess and the God, or the Lord and the Lady. Others in the path of Witchcraft follow many deities or focus just on one deity. However, there are also other witches who don't follow any deity figures at all, who don't believe in deity or are agnostic. Some see deity simply as the forces of nature and have no need to personify them or worship them in any way. If working with deity doesn't appeal to you, then please feel free to skip this chapter completely.

The deities within Hedge Witchcraft are the cycle and manifestation of nature that flows through each season, with no beginning and no ending. It is an endless turning of the tides, the times in our lives and in the world around us. The Goddess is often seen as the loom upon which the warp and weft of all life is made, and the God is seen as the manifestation of her energy. The Goddess is life and death and rebirth itself; she is the cycle. The God, like us, is bound to her and the cycle, showing us how to work with it in honour of her and all life.

How you decide to honour deity in your practice is your choice. You can choose to honour named deities with respect to their stories, the pantheon that they may belong to, and the culture that they were honoured in. You can certainly venerate deities from all over the world in your practice, but please respect their individual stories.

We will now look at the dual aspect of deity in the form of the Goddess and the God, their reflection in nature, and how they work together.

The Goddess and the God

In many traditions of modern Witchcraft, deity is split into two aspects: the God and the Goddess. We honestly don't know if our ancient ancestors believed in a goddess and a god, though many have speculated on this concept. Many correspondences are made with both the Goddess and the God, their symbology and their stories, and here we will take a look at some of these to broaden our perspective. Note that you may or may not agree with all of these associations, and you may come from a religious background that has differing opinions regarding these aspects, which is perfectly fine. Below I present a general and broad understanding, as well as my own perspective, of the Goddess and the God.

The Goddess

The Goddess is seen as the divine feminine. We see this reflected in everyday language, with many references to people referring to Mother Nature or to the earth as Gaia (a personification of the earth in Greek mythology). She is nurturing, giving of herself so that the world may continue, holding the balance within her hands. For even as she gives, she is also that which we return to upon death, and into the arms of the Great Mother we go before that energy is transformed into something new. She gives and receives, and we honour her for the many gifts in our lives. We know that we must treasure and nurture her, even as she nourishes us, for to do otherwise spells not only our doom but perhaps that of the entire planet. As children of the Goddess, we are all connected; we are all related.

The Goddess may be broken down into more specific attributes depending upon the person working with or worshipping her. She is often seen as goddess of the moon or goddess of the seas and oceans. She is the goddess of the earth, the land, the fertile fields, and agriculture. She is the goddess of the stars and the inky blackness of the night skies. She is the goddess of magic and Witchcraft.

The Goddess is the cycle. She is not beholden to the cycle of the seasons of nature and the earth itself, for she is the cycle. The God is the change belonging to and bound by her cycle, as we will see below.

Sometimes the Goddess is known as the Lady or the Dame. She is the energy of the universe, that which is flowing through all life. To use my loom analogy again, she is the loom that the web of life is woven upon, the great matrix of being. As such, she is unchanging, whereas the god, that which is woven through her, changes as different colours and threads are added throughout the year, until finally he is released from the loom itself. Think of the moon: the moon itself is unchanging; it is a round lump of rock orbiting our planet. It is through the reflection of sunlight and our own perspective here on earth that the phases of the moon seem to change. It is through the relationship of sun and moon that we see "change," even as we know that the moon itself is actually unchanging. She is the energy; he is the manifestation of that energy. She is the cycle; he is bound to that cycle. The Goddess is the mystery, the ethereal energy behind all life. The God teaches us to quest for that mystery.

The God

The God is the divine masculine, the polarity energy to that of the Goddess energy. Where the Goddess is often symbolised by the moon, the God is often symbolised by the sun. We follow the course of his life through the eight sabbats: the festivals, celebrations, and holy days of the witches. We see his journey from birth and infancy to old age and death throughout the cycle of a year.

He is the God of the Sun and the Lord of the Wildwood. He is often seen as an antlered god, symbolising his connection to the animal realms. Many traditions refer to him as the Horned God, yet depict him with antlers. This is a particular bugbear for this author, as there is a very specific difference between antlers and horns. Antlers are cyclical: they grow and then drop off in a continuous yearly cycle, usually in the males of deer species (with female reindeer being the exception). The antlered god represents the cycle of the seasons in this regard. Horned gods such as Pan are connected to nature, but the horns do not symbolise the same thing as antlers. Horns are grown and then they stay put unless they are broken. Horned gods represent the wild, nature, and animals for certain; however, they are still different to the symbolism found with an antlered god. Both horned gods and antlered gods are appropriate for Witchcraft; just make sure you know which is which in order to honour him properly!

The God is also associated with mountains (high places), crops such as wheat and barley, and the seasons. Some witches also honour the Oak King and Holly King, which are seasonal representations of the God's energy. At the solstices or sometimes at the festivals of Beltane and Samhain, the power of one king is taken over by the other.

Where the Goddess is the energy behind creation and all life, the God is the manifestation of that energy. If the Goddess is energy, the God is matter, bringing form to her energy. As she spins the threads of existence, it is through the God that these threads are woven into a tangible form. While she is the energy of all life, he is the physical representation of all that life. He is sometimes known as the Lord, the Old Lad, the King of the Wildwood, Lord of the Greenwood, the Green Man, or through a dual aspect of the Oak and Holly King, among others.

As King of the Wildwood he represents all that is untamed—the essence of the wild itself. As the Oak and Holly King, he represents the cycles of dark and light in the year, or the seasons of summer and winter. Some groups that use the Oak and Holly King in their work see the change of power from one to another at the solstices. It's more common in modern traditional Witchcraft for the change of power to occur at the start of the seasons rather than midway through at the solstices. So, for example, the Oak King comes into power at the beginning of summer here in Britain, around Beltane or May Day, and the Holly King takes over at Samhain, or Hallowe'en. For me, this makes more sense. Others prefer to see the change of power at the equinoxes.

A Local Lord and Lady

Yet another way to work with deity is to simply find a local concept that reflects the natural phenomena around you that relates to a Lord and a Lady. So, for instance, in her book *Of Chalk and Flint*, Val Thomas speaks of the Lord and Lady of Norfolk.[20] Those who follow this tradition, often called the Nameless Tradition, see the Goddess and God as the Lady of the Chalk and the Lord of the Flint. This reflects the natural landscape of the area, wherein the type of soil that nurtures life is seen as the feminine aspect of deity; the natural abundance of flint, which is used for a multitude of purposes, is seen as the masculine aspect of deity. Your local Lord and Lady will most likely be different, as your local area will have its own attributes that signify the deities of that area.

The Cycle of the Goddess and God

One way to honour deity in Witchcraft is to follow the cycle of the Goddess and God and their relationship to each other as represented through nature and natural phenomena. In this way, we see the God as a cyclical deity that is birthed, matured, and then dies to the Goddess every year.

At the darkest time of the year, at the winter solstice, the God is born of the Goddess. During the seasons of Imbolc and Ostara, the God grows as the Goddess begins to awaken life around them. The growing sunlight with each and every day is related to the growth of the God. At Beltane, when the young God and Goddess have reached maturity, they join together under the stars, and through their union the fertility abounds in the fields

20 Thomas, *Of Chalk and Flint*.

and hedgerows, the forests and the meadows. At midsummer we see both the God and the sun, his symbol, reach their peak of strength, after which both will lessen with each day as the sunlight wanes towards the dark half of the year again. The God's full strength has been given to the Goddess and into the crops, flora, and fauna that is their blessing. Through the seasons of Lammas and Mabon we see the God weakening, his life force going into the ripening grains, fruits, and other harvests. We see this reflected in the folklore and the old songs such as "John Barleycorn," wherein the tale of the God's cycle is told as he gives his energy to the barley. The Goddess feels the life stirring within her, the seed of the God also ripening. At Samhain the God dies to the world in the arms of the Goddess and manifests instead between the worlds, riding the night skies as the leader of the Wild Hunt. He is reborn of the Goddess again at Yule, being his own father even as the seed of the barleycorn begets its own.

All in all, there are so many different ways to work with deity. Choose a way of working with deity that has deep resonance for you. A deity must appeal to you, and the myths and cycles of their lives must make sense to you, otherwise you are missing a part of the mystery. It is in our quest to understand the deities that one of the main mysteries of Witchcraft is revealed: a true understanding of the ways of nature.

• • •

Below are some very brief examples of specific goddesses and gods that are honoured in the Craft, particular to the Celtic deities and the faery lore of the region. This list is by no means complete (in pantheon or deity) but offers a glimpse into some of the pantheons of deity that you might discover in the Craft. There are certainly many other pantheons and deities from all over the world found in the Craft. You might find resonance with some of the deities listed below, and I heartily encourage you to research everything you can about a deity that you would choose to work with. It is important to fully understand the divine power that you are going to be working with in your Craft.

As well, named deities such as those below have their own stories stemming from their own mythology, and therefore cannot and should not be squeezed into the story cycle of the Goddess and the God mentioned previously. Freya and Freyr from the Norse pantheon, whose names actually mean Lady and Lord, cannot be superimposed upon the cyclical relationship between the God and Goddess because their own personal stories are different. Freya doesn't give birth to Freyr at the winter solstice; in fact, they are brother and sister. Freyr doesn't die each year; he dies at Ragnarok. If you are working with named deities, go with their stories rather than the cyclical story of the divine feminine and divine masculine (otherwise simply known as the Goddess and the God) that explains the natural seasonal cycle. Named deities may be god forms of this divine energy, but they are individual and have their own mythologies.

Celtic Gods and Goddesses

ARIANRHOD: Lady of the Silver Wheel (the moon) and of the starry heavens

BELENUS: Gallic god of the sun, light

BRIGID: Known throughout Celtic lands under various epithets, this goddess is namely one of healing, smithcraft, and poetry, but she also has many other attributes

CERNNUNOS: Gallic lord of wild animals, the underworld

CERIDWEN: Welsh goddess of inspiration and initiation

DAGDA: Irish father god of magic and fertility

DANU: Irish mother goddess with water associations

GWYN AP NUDD: Welsh god and ruler of the otherworld (Annwn) and King of the Faeries

LUGH: Irish god also known as the "many skilled one," in whose name the sabbat of Lughnasadh is derived (the games/gathering of Lugh)

MORRIGAN: Irish goddess of battle and also healing/regeneration

RHIANNON: Welsh goddess of sovereignty, with horse associations and also faery connotations, as she initially appeared from the otherworld

TARANIS: Gallic god of thunder

Faery Gods and Goddesses

AINE: Irish goddess of Faery and of sovereignty

ARAWN (ARAWEN): Welsh king of the otherworld realm of Annwn, later conflated with Gwyn ap Nudd (see below)

CERNUNNOS: Celtiberian god of fertility, life, animals, and the underworld

COINCHEND: Gallic female warrior from the otherworld

GWYN AP NUDD: Welsh Lord of the Wild Hunt, King of the Fair Folk

RHIANNON: Welsh goddess of Faery and sovereignty

• • •

Please note that these attributes are only the tip of the iceberg when dealing with deities. They are not "job descriptions" but areas in which these deities have specific power or in which they flourish, in combination with others in their pantheon. They are also so much more than their attributes, as you will find if you begin working with them. You may discover new attributes and symbols that are not recorded, which are revealed to you through your deep relationship with them.

> *Always remember that the gods are so much*
> *more than the labels we give them.*

We label things in order to understand them, but we must remember not to confine things with labels or confuse them. The gods are so much more than us.

Prayer

Deity in the Craft is a very personal thing. The best way to get to know more about a deity, apart from extensive research, is through prayer. Some people have difficulty with the word *prayer*, seeing connotations to other religions from which they prefer to disassociate themselves. However, prayer is not relegated to certain religions and is found the world over. It is not solely a Christian practice or only pertaining to any of the other Abrahamic faiths. How else would we communicate with deity, whether it is a pre-Christian Irish goddess or Greek god of the sun or a god and goddess of our local area with no recorded historical name? If you are communicating with a deity, that is prayer.

Prayer can be simple or complex. You can recite long, flowery verses in loving devotion within a ritual to the gods of your choice or you may choose to honour them with a few simple heartfelt words throughout the day. How you choose to pray is entirely your decision.

Prayer is simply opening up a line of communication with deity. As Tennyson wrote, "More things are wrought by prayer than this world dreams of."[21] When we begin to establish a connection with deity, we find a growing relationship that flows both ways. We can talk to the deities and they can respond in turn. There are many ways to pray, such as:

- prayers of thanksgiving and gratitude

- prayers of devotion and love

- prayers of petition, such as asking for healing or guidance

- daily prayers to keep up a connection to deity throughout the day

- seasonal prayers recited in honour of the sabbats and the Wheel of the Year

Your prayers might be spontaneous, with words inspired by the beauty of nature spoken aloud or quietly in your mind to the gods and goddesses.

---

21 Tennyson, *Idylls of the King*.

You might find beautiful written prayers in books and literature that you wish to recite or memorise for ritual or daily practice. Old prayers are not necessarily better than new prayers. As well, writing your own prayers might have more relevance to your own practice than reciting the words of others. If you are feeling poetic, try writing your own prayer to deity after doing thorough research on their attributes, their likes and dislikes, their form and personality. You can then write your prayer around those ideas.

Here is an example of a prayer that I wrote to the Welsh goddess Arianrhod:

> *Lady of the Silver Wheel*
> *Whose realm of the starry heavens*
> *Glitters in silver and in gold*
> *Whose gifts of prophecy and sovereignty*
> *Are shared amongst your devoted*
> *Lady of magic*
> *You challenge me as you yourself have been challenged*
> *And I rise*
> *I rise*
> *I rise to the challenge*
> *To be my most authentic self*
> *With your guidance and wisdom*
> *Now and forever more*

This prayer takes into consideration her connection to the moon, her abilities, and also her stories as told through the Welsh myths. It is written plainly, without rhyming or meter. If you prefer to use rhyming and meter, this is also a good choice, for prayers are easier to memorise in that fashion.

For example:

> *Ceridwen, Ceridwen*
> *Brewer of the Awen*
> *Lend strength and protection*
> *Ceridwen, Ceridwen!*

When engaging in prayer, it is important to consider that there really *is* someone on the other end, and that being does not wish to be continually petitioned for things without getting anything in return. If we are constantly asking things of the gods, then imagine what it would feel like if someone was constantly petitioning you for help. The gods help those who help themselves. There is no problem with prayers of petition as long as they are balanced with other forms of prayer, perhaps daily prayer or prayers of gratitude.

Know that when we are petitioning the gods, we are not handing over our fates to them or asking them to solve all our problems. It is still up to us to instigate the change that is needed in our lives. We can petition the gods for help and guidance, but we must also do the hard work that is necessary to the task. We practice an independent tradition based upon personal responsibility. After all, that's why we are witches! And as witches, we pray to the deities as often as possible, both in ritual and outside of ritual, to keep that connection and relationship strong.

Lastly, it's important to allow space for the gods to talk to us and respond to our words. Prayer isn't just us talking to the gods; it's also about us listening to them.

• • •

If you choose to work with deity, then take your time to explore the Goddess and the God and deity or deities in general. Research all that you can about them, find out about local deities of the land where you live (while being careful not to appropriate another's tradition; always work *with* any indigenous peoples with their permission). Hedge Witchcraft is rooted in local tradition, so if you would like to define the Goddess and God more specifically to your area, this is a great thing to do to bring it even closer to home. If working with the feminine and masculine energies is enough, you may simply see them as Goddess and God. In your own tradition you may even find out new names for the energies of the Goddess and the God that are present in your area. For example, you might see the energies shifting with the seasons, and so have a light aspect and a dark aspect, or a summer/winter aspect to the Goddess and God, as mentioned previously. You might work with the Lady of the Earth and the Lord of the Sun or the Lady of Fruitfulness and the Lord of the Corn in the summer, or light half of the year. You might work with the Lady of the Deep Snows and the Lord of the North Wind for the winter, or dark half of the year. You might work with the Faery gods and goddesses that cross the boundaries from the otherworld into your own lands, or the Oak and Holly Kings. Witchcraft as a whole is so wonderful in that so many deities and differing forms of deities can work within a tradition; that is perhaps its greatest appeal.

Find out bit by bit how *you* see the deities; you don't have to do this or decide it all at once. It is better to go slowly, and don't forget: you can always ask the gods for guidance. Write down how you feel deity appears to you in your life, and go from there. Research all that you can on any deities that appeal to you. Call upon their old names deep in the heart of the forest or by the seashore in the heat of the noonday sun or under the light of the moon. Honour them and the Old Ways sincerely, from the heart, and you can't go wrong.

*Connecting with deity can bring a whole
other perspective to your Craft. May the
Lord and Lady bless you in your work.*

*S*he reaches her arms up and stretches her hands out towards the moon. The silvery light is bright, and it fills her soul with a cool reassurance. "My Lady of the Moon," she begins, reciting her prayer to the Goddess and connecting with her under the full moon. She feels the Goddess within her and all around her and knows that she walks with the Goddess each and every day. Just as the moon lights up the night, so too does her Goddess guide the hedge witch through the darkness. An owl hoots in the ash trees, and then the pheasants—half a dozen of them along the lane at the back of the hedge— call out in the still night. The sound echoes in the silence of night, an almost clarion call that causes the hedge witch's heart to beat faster and her breath to quicken. The Goddess is here. She knows it; they all know it. Her heart sings out to her Lady under the moon, joining the chorus.

It was a very special night.

5

The Lunar
Path

Moonlight drowns out all
but the brightest stars.

· · · · · · ·

J. R. R. Tolkien,
The Lord of the Rings

The moon is perhaps the most magical draw to the path of Witchcraft, and it is no different for hedge witches. To stand under the moonlight is to partake in a liminal experience, for though there is darkness all around, we are surrounded by a mysterious light, one which is not light in the usual sense but reflected light. It is light from an object that does not have its own inherent source; it is light from what would otherwise be darkness. It is a companion to hedge witches in their work.

By its silvery light the world is changed, made mysterious and beautiful with darkness around its edges. The moon is utterly enchanting as we watch it move through its phases, from dark to full and back to dark again. Within the cycle of the moon we can see the cycle of our lives. Yet, like all things on this planet, the moon does not operate independently. Its light is a reflection of the sun, and it is held in place by the earth's gravitational pull. The moon pulls as well, causing the high and low tides and swelling the world's seas and oceans with its magnetic draw. So too are we pulled by the energy of the moon from high to low, from dark to light, dancing in its energy.

Witches have always been associated with the moon. They were said to gather under the light of the full moon for their sabbaths and honour moon goddesses with devotional rites. The play of darkness and light with the moon's energy appeals to many a witch who honours both the light and the dark in their life. There are many deities associated with the moon and many cycles from various cultures around the world that follow a lunar-based schedule, whether it is for planting or reaping crops or creating a calendar that honours each of the thirteen moons in a year's cycle.

The Moon's Cycle

The moon's monthly cycle is roughly twenty-eight days, waxing from dark to full and back to dark again. (*Waxing* means growing larger, *waning* means growing smaller.) As well, the moon takes around the same amount of time to rotate on its own axis, which is why we don't see the moon spinning and hence why we never see the dark side of the moon. This is known as tidal locking.

The dark moon is when the moon is closest to the sun during the day (from our perspective here on Earth) and therefore we cannot see it at all. The angle of the sun when viewed from Earth is such that no reflective surface on the moon is visible. The new moon, which occurs two to three days after the dark moon, is the barest slip of a crescent that appears in the evening sky in the west shortly after sunset. This is when the first reflective surface of the moon becomes visible, with the horns of the crescent pointing to the left. The moon waxes to the first quarter about a week after the dark moon (otherwise known as a half moon), when the horns of the crescent disappear. From the half moon, the moon continues to wax to the full point, and in this phase it is called a waxing gibbous moon. *Gibbous* is from the Latin *gibbus*, which means "hump," and we can clearly see this growing bulge on the left-hand side of the moon where the horns of the crescent were.

The moon then reaches full, riding at its highest point in that cycle and also rising in conjunction with the sunset. This is the time of the fullest surface of the moon reflecting the sun's light, as they are at opposite ends of the planet from the earth's perspective.

We then see the waning phase of the moon's cycle, from waning gibbous, where the bulge is decreasing from the right-hand side, to the waning half-moon and then the waning crescent moon (with the horns of the crescent on the right-hand side).

The dark moon comes once again, where the moon seems to disappear from the night sky for three days—which, in fact, it does: it's in the sky during the daylight hours. A blue moon is when there are two full moons appearing in the same astrological sign. Nowadays people often refer to a blue moon as the second full moon in a calendar month, but this is technically incorrect.

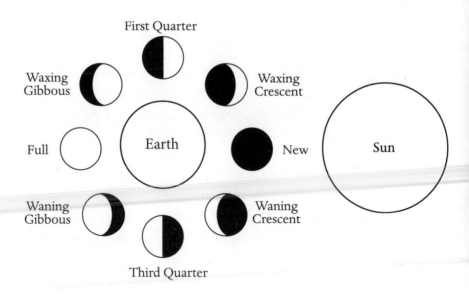

DIAGRAM 1: The Moon Phases[22]

22 Not to scale; the sun is 109 times larger than Earth!

If we observe the moon's rising and setting, we will note that it rises and sets at a different point each day, just as the sun does on the horizon. The moon's cycle is much quicker and more dramatic, travelling eastwards around thirteen degrees every day and rising approximately 50 minutes later each night. As the sun and moon are in a constant dance with each other, we see the cycles of the sun in the moon and the moon in the sun. Where the full moon rises at the winter solstice is where the sun rises at the summer solstice, for the longest night is then swapped with the longest day; the monthly moon cycle literally reflects that phenomenon. This event is swapped six months later. At each point where the full moon rises, in six months' time that is where the sun will rise.

When the moon is dark, it rises and sets with the sun. In the first quarter, when the moon is half, it rises at noon and sets at midnight. At the full moon, it rises at sunset and sets at sunrise. At the fourth quarter, the waning half moon, it rises at midnight and sets at noon.

• • •

Eclipses are yet another dance of the sun and moon with the earth. The dark moon blocks out the light of the sun during a solar eclipse. A solar eclipse can only happen when it is a dark moon.

A partial or full lunar eclipse is when the moon passes through the earth's shadow as cast by the sun. This can only occur when the moon is full as the sun needs to be on the opposite side of the earth for this phenomenon to happen.

The Moon and the Tides

As previously mentioned, the moon affects the tides, especially at the full and dark moons. When it is timed with the full or dark moon, we have what are known as spring tides, which are very high tides that, when combined with the weather, can create devastating storm surges. Despite the name, spring tides have nothing to do with the season and occur all year round. The full moon is also the time when you have the lowest tides, which often reveal surprising phenomenon along the coastline. A neap tide is the tide just after the first or third quarters of the moon when there is the least difference between high and low water. You can use tidal energy in spellcraft, meditation, and a host of other practices in your tradition.

One of the most liminal places for the hedge witch to work is by the shoreline, in a place that is neither the sea nor the land but an in-between place of constant flow and change.

Working with the Moon

Some work their Craft according to astrological timings with the moon, following what sign the moon is in and knowing that the sun is in the opposite sign at each full moon. The moon is in each astrological sign for approximately 2.5 days, and when the moon has made its last major aspect to a planet but has yet to enter a new sign, it is termed *void of course*. This is a phenomenon that can last a few hours to a day or more. Some witches will not do spellcraft or other work when the moon is void of course; others do not follow astrological tides at all. It is purely your choice as to how you wish to honour the lunar cycles in your own Craft. I personally follow the simpler phases of the moon, rather than astrological timings.

There are also many different names for the various moons throughout the yearly cycle, and perhaps the most famous of all is the Coligny calendar, a Gallic lunar calendar dating back to the second century. Indeed, we derive the word *month* from the word *moon*, and so following a lunar calendar in our Craft makes perfect sense. Each month it can help us attune not only to the cycle of the moon, but to what is happening in nature all around us at that particular moon. In the Coligny calendar, there is debate as to when each month started: whether it was the full moon, the new or dark moon, or starting from the sixth night of the waxing moon.

Month	Days	Etymology	Time Period
Samonios	30	Seed-fall	October/November
Dumannios	29	Darkest Depths	November/December
Riuros	30	Cold Time	December/January
Anagantios	29	Stay At Home Time	January/February
Ogronios	30	Time of Ice	February/March
Cutios	30	Time of Winds	March/April
Giamonios	29	Shoots Show	April/May
Simivisionios	30	Time of Light/Brightness	May/June
Equos	29/30	Horse Time	June/July
Elembiuos	29	Claim Time	July/August
Edrinios	30	Arbitration Time	August/September
Cantios	29	Song Time	September/October
Mid-samonios	30		Intercalary[23]

There are other lunar calendars used in the Craft, such as the Medieval English moon names, which may begin on either the dark or the full moon, depending upon how you wish to use them:

January: Wolf Moon	July: Grain Moon
February: Lenten Moon	August: Fruit Moon
March: Egg Moon	September: Harvest Moon
April: Milk Moon	October: Hunter's Moon
May: Flower Moon	November: Moon Before Yule
June: Hay Moon	December: Yule Moon[24]

Finding your own name for the full moons and lunar tides can have great meaning to your Craft. You may like to use names that reflect what is happening in your local area at the time. For instance, if you don't live in an area where corn or barley grow, you might like to change the name of the August and September moons to reflect a local phenomenon. For example, where I grew up in the mountains in Quebec, there was very little

23 Matthews, *Elements of the Celtic Tradition*, 92.
24 "The Names of the Moons," University College London.

farming in that mountainous, rocky soil. August was the time of thunderstorms, so I would name the August moon the Thunder/Lightning Moon. Alternatively, you could use the old names to honour the ancestral tides if you have ancestral ties to certain areas. Naming the moons makes it more personal and allows us to fully immerse ourselves in the lunar energies. It makes working with the lunar cycles something that is completely your own, unique to your own hedge witch tradition and your locality.

Rituals that take place during certain moon times—indeed, at any other time other than the solar-orientated sabbats—are called *esbats* in modern Witchcraft. So, we might perform a full moon esbat, or a full moon ritual, in our Craft. This comes from the French term *s'esbattre*, which means "to frolic."[25] There will be an example of a full moon esbat/ritual in chapter 13.

The Moon and Our Own Cycles

In all forms of Witchcraft, we feel the cycles of the moon in our blood and in our bones. Our energy often reflects those cycles, with the dark moon being a time of introspection and quiet, while the full moon can be a time of celebration and high energy. Many women see the twenty-eight-day cycle of the moon reflected in their menses, with the dark moon energy equating to the bleeding time, the waxing moon the building of uterine lining, the full moon as ovulation, the waning moon as the breakdown of uterine lining, and back to the dark moon and the bleeding time once again. Of course, a woman may bleed at any time of the moon; the above is just a correspondence with regard to women's menstrual cycles.

We can also see the moon in the cycle of a person's life, from birth, infancy and early childhood to teenage years, then maturity and middle age to old age and death. Many witches are now honouring all four phases of the moon, which includes the dark moon, and may prefer to follow a maiden, mother, queen, and crone version of the cycle of the Goddess where from the 1950s a triple goddess figure was honoured (maiden, mother, crone). Triple goddesses in many ancient myths and tales were

25 Murphy-Hiscock, *Solitary Wicca for Life*, 140.

sisters, not of different generations, and so this triple moon goddess of maiden, mother, and crone is seen as a modern invention, as is the later quadruple version. If either of these appeal to you, then by all means use them. It's your Witchcraft. You may also honour different goddesses at different times of the moon; for instance, the Celtic goddesses Andraste at the dark moon, Rhiannon at the waxing moon, Arianrhod at the full moon, and Ceridwen at the waning moon.

Goddesses of the Moon

There are many goddesses of the moon in Witchcraft, although in Pagan traditions across the world the moon isn't always associated with the female aspect, nor the sun with a male aspect. In Ireland the sun was viewed as a female divinity, and in Norse traditions the moon was male. In Witchcraft the majority, however, associate the moon with the divine feminine, and so here are some goddesses that are found in the various traditions. Please note that this is only a short list of the most popular; there are many, many other goddesses across the globe that are associated with the moon.

ANDRASTE: Sometimes known as Andred, this is a Celtic goddess associated with battle and protection as well as with divination and, more recently, the moon. She was most famously called upon by the Iceni queen Boudicca for divine retribution against her enemies from Rome. The name Andraste equates with Victory or the Invincible or Indomitable. Her moon association may be a modern interpretation, as there is no historical evidence available at the moment; however, you never know what will be uncovered in years to come. I have personally found that she is particularly strong at the dark moon.

ARADIA: Daughter of the Roman moon goddess Diana, she taught Witchcraft to humanity.

ARDUINNA: Gallic goddess of the moon, the forest, and hunting. The boar was her sacred animal.

ARIANRHOD: A Welsh goddess often known as the Lady of the Silver Wheel, from the Welsh *arian*, "silver," and *rhod*, "wheel." Her fortress, Caer Arianrhod, is connected with a rock formation visible off the coast of northern Gwynedd at low tide.

ARTEMIS: A Greek goddess usually associated with the maiden and sometimes even with darker, more violent aspects, including sacrifice. She is usually depicted as a classical goddess with lunar associations but mostly as a chaste huntress.

DIANA: Roman goddess of the moon whose name is associated with the sky and daylight.[26] Often referred to as Queen of the Witches.

HECATE: This Greek goddess's triple aspect has perhaps been the greatest inspiration for the modern triple goddess aspect of the moon.

LUNA: Roman goddess of the moon, sometimes part of a triplicate with Proserpina and Hecate.

SELENE: The Greek goddess who drives her moon chariot across the sky.

The Moon and the Hedge Witch

The hedge witch works with the cycles of the moon, feeling them in everything that they do, flowing through their day and night. They know that the power of the moon is reflected in everything, even as the moon reflects the light of the sun. The moon is a mirror that reflects our soul's truths back to us, where we can shine in the darkness and honour our own seasons of waxing and waning.

With all the flows of energy in nature, the hedge witch works with the tides, the currents that swirl around us in eddies and whorls, shaping and changing our lives. We know that to work *with* the current, instead of against it, helps us in every aspect of our daily living. We research the lore

---

26 Encyclopaedia Britannica, "Diana: Roman Religion."

accorded to the moon's cycles and pay attention to the lunar tides, knowing that the best time for weeding the garden is during the fourth quarter to dark moon, and the best time to plant root vegetables is the third quarter. During the first and second quarter we will sow the seeds of aboveground crops, using the waxing lunar energies to their full benefit. We will mow the lawn during the waning moon so that we will not have to mow it again soon. We will work our Craft according to the moon, honouring the full and dark moons with ritual and working spellcraft in accordance with the moon's phases. Women see the moon reflected in their own menstrual cycle (should they have one) and note the timings in accordance with the moon. We know, as hedge witches, that all this is not absolutely necessary, but we also know full well the power of cycle and of paying attention.

And above all, our hearts dance
under the light of the moon.

It is a cold winter's night, the full moon riding high in the sky. Everything is sharply outlined in the clear silver light. There is an eldritch glow to the entire back garden. A faint tingle runs down the hedge witch's spine. She knows that the Faery Raede will soon pass by under the light of the moon and that she must wrap up her work to leave them in peace. She bows her head to the beautiful shining orb and makes her way through the moon shadows across the lawn to leave an offering. She can feel the pulse of the lunar energies flowing through her body, cleansing, healing, and awakening the enchantment of her soul. She gives her thanks for these blessings, then turns with a final look at the moon before heading back inside. The garden, silent under the silver light, awaits even more magic…

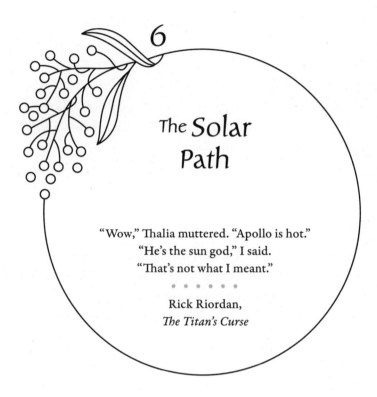

6

The Solar Path

"Wow," Thalia muttered. "Apollo is hot."
"He's the sun god," I said.
"That's not what I meant."

• • • • • •

Rick Riordan,
The Titan's Curse

Just as witches follow the tides of the moon, so too do they follow the cycles of the sun. The sun is the light of life, a great power that controls the green and growing things. Witches all over the world feel the strengthening and weakening tides of the sun in their hearts and souls. Hedge witches pay particular attention to the length of days and through careful observation know where the sun rises and sets in their local area throughout the year. They may spend many mornings and evenings watching the sunrise and sunset from the same vantage point so that they can pull together all their solar knowledge and make it applicable to their Craft.

The tides of the sun are reflected in the eight sabbats found in modern Witchcraft. We follow the path of the sun in the two equinoxes and the two solstices, as well as the four fire festivals that mark important timings in the agricultural/seasonal year as dictated by the sun's gifts, local weather, and rural phenomena.

The Wheel of the Year

The eightfold Wheel of the Year known in modern Paganism was created by Gerald Gardner and Ross Nichols, who were mentioned earlier. They may have been influenced by symbols of eight-spoked wheels that were found carved into rocks in various parts of Scandinavia alongside what we believe to be sunwheels. Gardner and Nichols brought together folklore and traditions from across Britain and Europe to create a system that had a festival around every six to eight weeks. In doing so, they found a way to connect to the natural world around them more fully via a system that honoured both solar and agricultural/seasonal phenomena. And, as we like to say in Witchcraft, if it works, use it!

This system was devised in the UK following UK seasonal shifts, though it contains elements found in other areas of Europe. If you don't live in the UK, you may adapt or follow a slightly different system to reflect what is happening in your local area. Or you might like to follow an ancestral link and use the British system wherever you are, feeling that this connects you to the energies and links you in with ancestral ties. In the Southern Hemisphere, many in the Craft have reversed the sabbats as this better reflects what is happening in their part of the world. Around December 21 they would celebrate the summer solstice as this is when they have their summer season.

As previously mentioned, there are four sabbats that honour the tides of the solstices and equinoxes and are directly related to the position of the sun, yet these signal the start of the seasons for many in North America. For example, the season of spring arrives much later in many parts of Canada than it does in most of the UK, so while many in Britain celebrate the first signs at the beginning of February, many across the Atlantic are still under several feet of snow, even at the astronomical timing of the spring equinox. In Canada the spring equinox is seen as the beginning of spring, whereas here in the UK it is towards the middle of our spring season, with May Day or Beltane as the start of summer. Our harvests are different, with different crops and timings. So, as a hedge witch, you will have to look closely at the land where you live and see how you can adapt anything that isn't quite working with the energies where you live.

*Many within the Craft equate the sabbats
with the masculine and the energy of the
sun, and therefore weave the tale of the Sun
God into their cosmology and mythos, telling
how the cycles of the seasons rise and fall.*

The Sabbats

The names of the sabbats, or solar festivals, are a mix of Celtic and Northern European/Germanic words. This is because there is no intact tradition that has been handed down throughout the centuries, so modern Paganism and Witchcraft have pieced together the puzzle as best they can to reflect the energies of the solar and agricultural tides with the words and traditions that best describe them. In the UK there has been such a blending of different cultures, from our Stone Age ancestors through to Celtic, Norse, Saxon, Danish, French, and other cultures influencing not only the religion, but the language in these isles. Witches, being of such diverse traditions, may follow the mythos of the relationship between the God and Goddess as reflected in the natural world or may have their own mythos and local language to reflect what is happening seasonally around them. It is an ever-growing and evolving life path.

YULE: around December 21 (Winter Solstice)—Germanic

IMBOLC: around February 1 (Candlemas)—Celtic

OSTARA: around March 21 (Spring Equinox)—Germanic

BELTANE: around May 1 (May Day)—Celtic

LITHA: around June 21 (Summer Solstice)—Old Saxon
(West Germanic)

LUGHNASADH: around August 1 (First Harvest)—Celtic (also known as the Anglo-Saxon/West Germanic Lammas)

MABON: around September 21 (Autumn Equinox)—Celtic (a modern Celtic term)

SAMHAIN: around October 31 (Hallowe'en)—Celtic

You may also feel a desire to celebrate not by the calendar, but by the seasonal shifts themselves. Letting the natural world around you influence your celebrations and rituals is something that is deeply important to the Craft. It is also a practice that is based on locality; for instance, if at Imbolc you are still deep under five feet of snow, then perhaps celebrating the lambing season and the first snowdrops (as is traditional in Britain) doesn't resonate with you at all.

Each hedge witch's practice will be different because each is influenced by their own experience, knowledge, and locality. You may not even use the titles given to the eight festivals in the Wheel of the Year at all. You may work with the lunar tides and create festivals that honour what is happening around you at each moon's cycle. Or, if the natural world around you describes four or five festivals, then feel free to go with that if you so desire. It is perfectly acceptable to celebrate the first frost as the beginning of winter. For me personally here in the east of the British Isles, the eightfold Wheel of the Year does reflect what is happening in my part of the world. Witches living in the far north of Britain may celebrate the sabbats or their festivals a few weeks later, as spring arrives much earlier in the south and east of England than it does in the north of Scotland.

The solstices and equinoxes are times and tides that all can agree on, being fixed dates in the astronomical calendar. However, the agricultural/ seasonal festivals may have huge differences in timing. The lambing season here is usually around February, but some local farmers have it during December when they have the whole family on holiday to help out. It is fairly mild here in the east of England so close to the coast, so new grass is available at this time of year. In the north, though, this might not be the case. The cutting of the first crop of wheat can happen anytime mid-July to mid-August as it is very much weather dependent, needing enough rain in the months before to grow tall and strong, but also requiring dry weather in order to harvest.

> *Celebrating by the calendar can put us out of sync with nature sometimes, but there are other benefits. With so many Pagans celebrating at these specific times of the year, we can tap into the collective energies of these days and nights and ride those tides if we so wish. Again, it's your choice.*

Let's now look at each of the sabbats in more detail.

Samhain

We all know of the modern-day Hallowe'en that falls on October 31, but few outside of the Craft know of the origins of this festival. Samhain is a Celtic festival that celebrates the time when the veil between this world and the otherworld is thin, and we can connect more easily with the unseen, both in the form of the Fair Folk (faeries) as well as the ancestors. The Celts reckoned their days from sunset to sunset, so Samhain runs from sunset on October 31 to sunset on November 1. The Celts divided the year into two halves, the dark half and the light half, and we see this reflected in much of modern Witchcraft today. How this is divided depends on the tradition. If you are following one from Celtic lore, the dark half of the year begins at Samhain and ends at Beltane, when the light half of the year begins. This is the Celtic beginning of winter and summer, for they only considered two seasons in their worldview. *Samhain* means "summer's end." Other traditions of Witchcraft see the dark and light halves of the year commencing at the solstices with the myth of the Oak King and the Holly King. We will explore this later when we look at the solstices.

This may be the time when a new set of deities takes over from the previous set, in accordance with the season. In my area, for instance, at Samhain the mists begin to appear on the heath at sunset and shroud the area in the blessings of the Lady of the Mists. During the day, the antlered Lord of the Hunt or the Lord of the Wildwood is seen in the large winter herds of deer that gather together on the heathland, sometimes hundreds strong. I can feel a strong shift in the deity energy around me at this time of year, when the powers are handed over and a new season begins.

All around us at this time of year, the leaves are falling or have already fallen, and many of the fields that do not contain winter crops lie fallow. The bright colours of the flowers are gone, and the world becomes muted, softer, both to the eye and to the ear. The birds have flown in their migratory patterns, and the insects have either died or sought hibernation. It is a time of reflection, for the harvest is now over, and we can take stock of what we have reaped and what we have sown in our lives. In the fertility mythos, the Sun God fades into the west, his strength gone and the darkness of night closing in. He dies in the arms of the Goddess, to be reborn again at Yule. He then rides out to and fro from the otherworld as leader of the Wild Hunt, collecting the souls of those who have passed and taking them to their destination on the other side. He is the psychopomp.

Here in the UK, the days are especially short during this seasonal tide, with six to eight hours of sunlight (if it isn't raining, and even less in the northern parts) and many, many long hours of darkness afterwards. The winds outside are howling, the rain and hail patters on the windows, and the Wild Hunt rides. Some know the God as Gwyn ap Nudd, the lord of the underworld, riding at its head and collecting the souls of those who have died during the year, as well as any unwary travellers. We say good-bye to the warmth and light of summer and welcome the darkness and winter.

If we are working with the handover of power from one set of deities to another, we honour the energies of this shift in energy towards the dark half of the year. We may light a candle in the window to light the way for all those who have died in the year, or we might have a dumb supper, a meal taken in silence with a special plate for the ancestors to feast with us on this special night. Bobbing for apples brings us fortune in the coming year, for Samhain is also seen as the New Year in modern Witchcraft, when the cycle turns once again. The apple is a symbol of rebirth, and if we are lucky or skilled enough, we can capture it to bring us good fortune.

Yule (Winter Solstice)

The winter solstice occurs around December 21, give or take a day for the precise astronomical timing. It is the shortest day of the year and the longest night. For three days during the solstices (both winter and summer), the sun rises and sets in the same place on the horizon, suspending its travels southwards or northwards before reversing direction upon rising following the solstice. In the run-up to the winter solstice, the sun has travelled southwards along the horizon with each sunrise until it rises at its most southerly point at the solstice, where it rises in the same place for three days. After this it then begins to rise more northerly with each morning's sunrise and set further north as well with each sunset. During the solstice the sun "stands still," from the Latin *sol* ("sun") and *sistere* ("to stand still").

In some Witchcraft traditions, this is the time of the birth of the Sun God, who has risen again after his death at Samhain. The Goddess, impregnated at Beltane (some traditions use the spring equinox as the date of impregnation, nine months before, but hey, who says a goddess has a human cycle?) gives birth to the God again, and the cycle continues. The sun, after standing still for three days, now begins to gain in strength, and even as the Goddess rests, he continues to grow.

Others within the Craft see this time as the tide when the darkness gives way to light through the myth of the Oak King and Holly King. At the solstices the two kings battle for supremacy for half of the year; at the winter solstice, the Oak King wins out over the Holly King and the light half of the year begins. At the summer solstice, the Oak King loses his strength and the Holly King wins, beginning the dark half of the year. A battle between two kings is a common motif throughout Celtic folklore but in this interpretation is a more modern invention, being traced back to Robert Graves's work *The White Goddess,* with the myth inspired by some of the material in Sir James Frazer's *The Golden Bough* and his chapter "The Killing of the Tree Spirit."

For others, this is the time of the Wild Hunt during the twelve days of Yule. In Norse and Germanic traditions, Odin, Woden, or the goddess Holle ride through the sky at the head of the Wild Hunt.

In the southwest of Britain, the tradition of wassailing the orchards still continues to this day. It honours the apple trees (and other fruit trees, but mostly apple) by giving them a libation of cider and sometimes even shooting guns into their branches to scare away evil spirits (and possibly be a lazy form of pruning). Throughout Europe evergreens were also brought into the home, their foliage reminding us of the continuity of life and how the spirit never dies. Mistletoe, an herb that was sacred to the ancient druids, was used in Victorian times much as it is today, in the form of the kissing bough, with a berry picked for every kiss until there was none left.

Imbolc

Imbolc occurs around January 31–February 1 or 2, depending upon which tradition you follow. The Christian feast day of Candlemas falls on February 2, which is why some people celebrate it on this day, as it is a holiday that has melded Pagan and Christian traditions. Others who follow a more Celtic-based Pagan tradition celebrate this time from sunset on January 31 to sunset on February 1. This is known in Celtic lands as Brigid's Day, a time to honour the goddess Brigid. In Witchcraft we honour the returning light of the sun, and the returning warmth of spring from the Goddess. The God is growing stronger as the sun grows stronger with each day.

In the UK the first flowers of snowdrops are out and the land is beginning to warm up after the winter. Elsewhere, as in North America, many places may still be under a blanket of snow, so this is a quiet time of reflection and celebration of the lengthening days and the nourishment of the Goddess.

Imbolc comes from the Celtic word *oimelc*, which means "in the belly" or "ewes' milk."[27] At this time of year, traditionally the sheep would be giving birth, providing the people with much-needed fresh milk, from which they could make new butter and cheeses to last them through the difficult early spring tides, when food was scarce as the winter's stores ran low and new crops were yet to be seen. In the Craft we can celebrate this quiet time by honouring the Mother Goddess and the flow of new milk, as well as the strengthening light of the Sun God. Or we might see the Lord and Lady's powers reflected in the natural world around us at this time, releasing the hold of winter and coaxing a gentle tide of new life to the land.

Ostara (Spring Equinox)

Ostara comes from the Northern European goddess Ēostre, also from whom we get the term *Easter*. It is thought linguistically that this comes from the Proto-Indo-European root "to shine," from which we also get our word *east*. She is seen as a goddess of spring, fertility, dawn, and new beginnings, and the symbols of the season are hares and, of course, eggs.

Astronomically, this is the time when the hours of day and night are equal; there is balance between light and dark just before the tipping point over into the favour of longer days and shorter nights as we traverse the Wheel of the Year into the summer. The sun is growing ever stronger, the birds have changed their song, and the wild animals are all shifting from their winter behaviours. The Goddess walks the land in youthful beauty. The God is reaching maturity, beginning to seek out the Goddess. We see the play of balance and honour both the light and dark at this time of year.

The concept of balance was traditionally and playfully enacted during this time, when it is said that you are able to balance an egg on its end at the precise moment of the equinox (I have yet to succeed). Eggs would be a welcome sight at this time of year for our ancestors, whose hens had stopped laying over the long, dark nights of winter and who would have begun laying again at this time of year. Hares were held in high regard for

27 Hughes, *Natural Druidry*, 184.

the ancient Celts, and it was recorded by Julius Caesar that it was taboo to hunt them.[28] The chocolate eggs and bunnies of today are a reflection of these older memories.

This is an excellent time to watch the sun rise, for at this point it will rise due east and you can orientate yourself and your space to this direction for all your magical and mystical workings.

Beltane

Using the Celtic model, Beltane begins at sunset on April 30 and runs through to sunset on May 1. It is a magical time of year. To this day in Britain we still have the secular May Day, in which we have a bank holiday on the nearest Monday. Beltane is the time when the Goddess and God come together in joyous union, sharing their love for each other and, in doing so, seeing the fertility in all nature responding in kind. The birds are singing and nesting, the trees are in full blossom, and the celebration of life can be felt everywhere.

In many places in Britain, you will see maypoles being erected at this time of year. Though many believe these to be phallic representations of the virility of the God, there is another theory that is equally valid. Ancient Celts honoured sacred trees, and often the *bile,* or sacred tree (sometimes a pole), was erected in the centre of the village as a symbol of the strength and power of the community. Other neighbouring tribes would cut down the bile of the villages they were raiding, either to destroy or gain that power. The maypole could indeed be a remnant from this, symbolising the power and strength of the world tree, the axis mundi, the centre of the world, the centre of the people's power.

Beltane is another important liminal time, often seen as one of the three spirit nights where the hosts of faery ride out as the veils between this world and the otherworld are thin. The festivals of Beltane, Midsummer, and Samhain have particular importance for the hedge witch who works with the Fair Folk and the otherworld. As well, fire is a very important part

---

28 Krappe, "Old Celtic Taboos."

of this festival, as the bel-fires (Beltane fires) were lit on hilltops throughout the land to signal this time and tide. The Celtic god Belinus, the Shining One often considered to be a solar deity, is thought to be where we get the festival's name.

Beltane signalled the start of summer, and here in the UK it certainly still does today.

Summer Solstice (Litha/Midsummer)

Litha is an Anglo-Saxon word used in part to designate the months of June and July. These two months were recorded by Bede as *ærra līþa* (before Litha) and *æfterra līþa* (after Litha).[29] The word *litha* is a little obscure: in 725 CE we see Bede use the word to mean "'gentle' or 'navigable,' because in these months the calm breezes are gentle and they were wont to sail upon the smooth sea."[30] It could relate to the full moon nearest the solstice in this period and the monthly reckoning of before and after the full moon giving the months their names. It could also relate to the day of the summer solstice itself. Litha, or the summer solstice, occurs around June 21 but may shift a day or so from year to year, just as the winter solstice may.

At Litha—or the summer solstice or midsummer, as it is known here in the UK—the sun has reached its furthest north-eastern rising point, and its furthest northwestern setting point. Here, for three days, the sun will rise and set at these points on the horizon in the same place before beginning its journey southwards as the days begin to shorten. It is also when the sun reaches its highest point in the sky, giving us the longest day, and the nearest full moon will reach its lowest trajectory (reversed at the winter solstice). The God is at the height of his powers, and he sends that energy into the world.

Fire or sun-wheels were often rolled down hillsides to represent the sun's power at this time of year, and perhaps to bring that solar energy to the

---

29 Bede, *Bede: The Reckoning of Time*, 54.
30 Ibid.

land. The Fair Folk are often out riding the land, and many are the tales of humans encountering them at midsummer. It is a propitious time for all workings with the Fair Folk. In the mythos of the Oak King and the Holly King, this is when the Holly King wins the battle and takes over the power from the Oak King to rule during this half of the year. It is that point when the God's strength has reached its peak, just before the decline in the shortening of days.

Lughnasadh (Lammas)

Lughnasadh is a Celtic term used to denote the "Feast of Lugh" or "the Gathering of Lugh." At this time of year, the bright and shining god Lugh held a feast in honour of his foster mother, Tailtiu, who died providing for her people. The name *Tailtiu* comes from Old Celtic *Talantiu*, meaning "The Great One of the Earth."[31] By the calendar, this festival is celebrated on the eve of July 31–August 1.

Games and contests are traditional at this festival, and some are still held to this day in Celtic lands. In Wicca and modern Witchcraft, this festival honours the cutting of the first crop, usually wheat or barley. The Sun God is seen to have given his strength to the crops, and now begins the drying and dying off of the crops, where he slowly fades in strength and passes his energy through the crops and the seeds/grain. The other name for this festival comes from the Anglo Saxon *hloafmass* or loaf mass, celebrating the first grains in the baking of bread.

Mabon (Autumn Equinox)

Mabon is the modern Witchcraft name for the autumn equinox. In Welsh mythology Mabon is the son of Modron, and they are an example of a divine Mother Goddess and Son God duality. Mabon is a derivative of Maponus, a god who is often associated with the Greek Apollo and may have solar connotations. Indeed, Apollo Maponus and his separation from Matrona, the mother, is one of many wasteland myths where fertility

---

31 Freeman, *Kindling the Celtic Spirit*, 237.

is restored upon his return.[32] In Welsh mythology Mabon was stolen as a babe from his mother, and was later returned by Arthur, reuniting the masculine and feminine, as part of an even grander tale. Aidan Kelly used this mythology when he coined the term *Mabon* in 1974 for this festival.[33] In the Mabinogi, Mabon was "the greatest hunter," and even though Kelly does not use this in his explanation of the naming of the festival, it does also have relevance to this time of year in the northern hemisphere, where in many places it falls near the beginning of the hunting season.

In modern Witchcraft, this time is seen as the time when the Goddess is preparing while nature begins winding down; the approaching tides of winter are on the wind. The God is changing, giving the last of his energy into the harvest before returning to the Wildwood and his Hunter aspect.

Autumn equinox is the second "equal night," when the length of day and night are equal. It falls between September 20–22. Harvest Suppers and Harvest Home are still celebrated widely across many UK parishes, and they are similar in sentiment to Thanksgiving.

• • •

The eight sabbats take us on a journey through the natural world and the shifting of the seasons. That being said, the hedge witch doesn't just work on the sabbats and the esbats. The work of the hedge witch is in each and every moment of each and every day.

> *If we have begun to lose our way, the seasonal*
> *festivals and the lunar tides are times that*
> *remind us to reconnect to the natural world.*
> *In modern times perhaps this is even more*
> *important than it was for our ancestors.*

---

32 Parker, *The Four Branches of the Mabinogi.*
33 Kelly, "About Naming Ostara, Litha, and Mabon."

*T*he hedge witch walks through the old parish church decorated with flowers and foliage for Harvest Home. It smells wonderful in this old stone building, the scent of dried grasses and blossoms filling the air. She loves these old parish churches in very rural settings where one can just walk in and admire the handicraft of the pew carvings and the tales they tell of the stories of the land, monsters and the fey, saints and sins, and the wonderfully embroidered altar cloth covered in a vine and leaf design. The old tales are here still, and in this spot she knows that older ceremonies took place, before this church was built, here on the coast above the marshes. The stories are still held here in the old building, out on the land, and in the scent and beauty of the floral displays made by local groups that adorn the church. The hedge witch takes one last look at the empty, silent church and stands in the open doorway, looking out onto the graveyard and, further in the distance, the hazy blue-grey of the sea. This is a powerful place, a liminal place, a place where the sabbats and the seasons are still honoured and remembered, although in a different form. She smiles, then closes the heavy oaken door behind her.

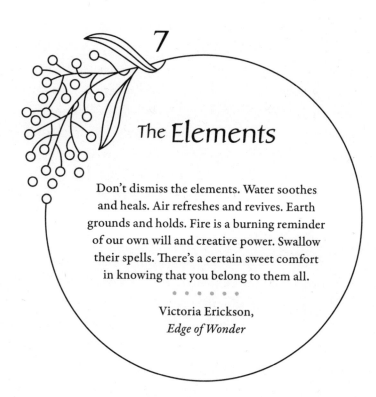

7

The Elements

Don't dismiss the elements. Water soothes
and heals. Air refreshes and revives. Earth
grounds and holds. Fire is a burning reminder
of our own will and creative power. Swallow
their spells. There's a certain sweet comfort
in knowing that you belong to them all.

• • • • • •

Victoria Erickson,
Edge of Wonder

In much of modern Witchcraft, you will hear about working with the elements, both in ritual and daily life. These elements are earth, air, fire and water. Stemming from ancient Greece and traced to the pre-Socratic philosopher Empedocles, these four elements were added to by Aristotle, who came up with a fifth element, called aether. Elemental systems can be found the world over, with slightly differing concepts. The above five elements form a method of viewing the world in Hinduism, for example, where the four elements of earth, air, fire, and water represent matter, and the fifth element represents spirit. In Celtic lands the elements were viewed as land, sea, and sky, with fire being the central point. The ancient Greek view of the four elements with the fifth element of aether persisted throughout the Middle Ages and into the Renaissance. Even today, the four elements can be linked to the scientific states of matter: solid, liquid, gas, and plasma.

Heinrich Cornelius Agrippa related spirits to the four elements but did not give them names. The Renaissance philosopher Paracelsus later attributed mythical beings to each of these four elements: gnomes were from the earth, sylphs from the air, salamanders from fire, and undines from water. These "elementals" are much worked with in the Craft today.

In the Craft, working with the elements helps us ground our practice and provide us with a set of correspondences so that we can work our magic. These are energies that we can tap into and acknowledge in our work, both within and without. When used in ritual, especially in circle casting, they ground and centre the magic circle, and in spellcraft they can lend their energies to our work (more on both of those later).

In modern Witchcraft we have a whole host of correspondences that help us work with the elements. Earth is associated with the direction of north, the darkest time of the year, and winter, the cold winds, midnight, and death. Air is associated with the direction of east, the time of spring when the world begins to green again, dawn and birth/infancy. Fire is associated with the south, the time of greatest light, the height of summer, noon, and maturity. Water is associated with the west, the twilight hours, and autumn, sunset, and old age. These are the classical correspondences, which may or may not work for you in your own locality. I will present the classical format first, then discuss how in my own practice I need to relocate some of the elements and their directions in order to fit in with my environment.

Earth

Earth is often seen as feminine, as we live upon Mother Earth. It is solid, a firm foundation for our lives and our work. It is the most tangible of the four elements. Earth is the ground upon which we walk. It is the soil in our gardens, the soil in which we grow our food. It is the tall mountains that reach up into the sky and the dark caves that reach deep into the earth. It is the green and growing things, the vegetation. It is food and nourishment. It is moist and fertile. It is cool and damp.

Earth is associated with the midnight sun in the depths of winter, the deep darkness of the darkest time of the year in the north. It is the quiet time when snows, frost, and ice cover the land, when the trees are laid bare against the grey and bleak skies and silence lies all around us in the sleeping countryside. It is also the tomb, the darkness of death that awaits us all at the end of our life's journey. It is the burial mounds and ancient tumuli that are said to be portals to the underworld, the otherworld of faery.

Earth is also abundance and prosperity. It rules over spellcraft involving money, new jobs, new homes, fertility, and abundance. Magic using stones, knots, poppets, and other images, as well as tree and herbal magic, is associated with earth. Spells will often include burying an item or sending energy into the earth or drawing it up from the earth. It works with the energies of stability, helping us ground and find our footing. It is the colour green and the black of night. The time is midnight and the stage in life is death, when we return to the Mother to be reborn once more in the darkest depths.

Some animals that are associated with earth are bear, badger, fox, hare, crow, cat, and owl. Gnomes are the mythological creatures associated with earth. In the tarot, the earth is associated with the suit of pentacles. The ritual tool is the pentacle, the five-pointed star set within a circle. Herbs associated with earth include barley, clover, fir, patchouli, pine, sage, and vervain.

Working with earth energies can help us ground and centre, then return to our sense of self. We can visualise roots growing out from beneath our feet or from the base of our spine as we sit upon the earth and ground ourselves in the deep, dark energy. We can also cleanse ourselves using the energy of earth simply by lying down on the ground and pushing out all negative energy into the earth, there to be transformed by the Goddess herself like the fallen leaves in autumn. We can also pull up lovely clean energy from the earth or ask a tree to share it with us as we lean against its trunk. We can use divination with different types and colours of stones or look into a patch of bare earth to see what symbols may appear to our minds.

An overabundance of earth energy in our lives can lead to stubbornness or lethargy. We can feel as if we have the weight of the world on our shoulders. We need to counter earth energies with the other elements, ideally holding them all in balance within ourselves. Often air is a good counterbalance to an overabundance of earth energy.

Working with the earth helps us find stability in our lives. It is cleansing and transformative in a slow, gentle way. It is also my favourite element, as rooting myself in the land is perhaps the most important part of my practice.

Air

Though we cannot see the element of air itself, we can see its effect on other things: the wind through the trees, the clouds in the sky, the colours of sunrise, the smoke rising from burning incense. Air is often thought of as a masculine element, as is fire. Feminine elements are seen as earth and water, though you may prefer not to associate any gender to the element at all; it's purely your choice.

Air is thought; it is the initial idea before something becomes manifest. It is therefore associated with new beginnings, learning, and academia. It is the blue sky and the rising sun; it is the tempest and the storm. It is music and the spark of inspiration. It is the air we breathe; it is our breath itself.

Air is the light of a new dawn, the rising sun in the east. It is springtime, when the buds are just beginning to open and the flowers and tree blossoms turn their faces to the sun. It is the time of love, romantic love and also friendship, even as the birds are singing their sweet songs to each other in courtship. It is adolescence and young adulthood, where we are finding our feet and experimenting with life. Its colours are white and yellow.

*Air is the huge expanse of skies over our head
and freedom within our souls. It is thought and
visualisation. In spellcraft it involves questing
for inspiration and new ideas, as well as travel
and experimentation. It is clear sight and
seeing through deceptions. It is often used in
communication spells. Some animals that are
associated with air are hawks, eagles, and birds
of all kinds, including the cockerel, as well as
bees, other winged creatures, and also spiders.*

The tool of air is something that is debatable in the Pagan community. Many see the tool of this element as the sword, while others see the wand as the element of air. The tarot suit of swords is air; however, Deborah Lipp gives us some more information on why this is when many see the wood of the wand as more connected to fire. Many see the heat of the forge as more connected to fire and the tool of the sword or athame (a ritual knife common to Wicca) than to air.[34] The Rider-Waite-Smith tarot is the most popular, hence the people who use it follow the elemental connections with the suits contained within the deck. However, A. E. Waite was a member of the Golden Dawn and had taken an oath of secrecy, and he made some changes so as not to devolve all of their secrets to the public at large. He didn't want to reveal everything from the order in the tarot deck, but he still wanted to keep some associations. Cups and pentacles were very much associated with water and earth respectively, so they couldn't easily be changed. However, swords and wands could! As the Golden Dawn associated air with wands and fire with swords, Waite figured he'd switch these associations in the tarot deck and thus keep some semblance of secrecy as per his oath to the order.

34 Lipp, *The Way of Four Spellbook.*

So, if you work with the tarot, you may have different associations than others who do not work so closely with the tarot. Personally, I prefer wands to correspond with the element of air and swords or the athame with fire, but that's my choice.

The magical creature associated with the element of air is the sylph. You can call upon these creatures as elementals in ritual to bring that element into play. Herbs that are associated with air include agrimony, aspen, birch, cedar, clary sage, clover, comfrey, hazel, mint, mistletoe, pine, and wormwood.

Too much of the air element in your life can lead to a feeling of disassociation, arrogance, a "head in the clouds feeling," or a lack of empathy. Balance that out with the stability of earth or the compassion of water.

Fire

We humans have such a fascination with fire. Perhaps because it is both life-sustaining and destructive at the same time, we see our own lives reflected in the flames. We are drawn to it like moths to a flame.

Our ancient ancestors are still with us, showing us the importance of fire. Fire is the birth of technology for our ancestors. Learning to work with fire brought us better tools as well as warmth and light in the darkness. We still feel that kinship with our ancestors when we gather around a fire, the hypnotic flames enticing us to look deeper into ourselves and the world. There is a mysticism associated with fire that has been shown in ancient fire temples and rituals around the world.

Magically speaking, fire is masculine in nature, and it is probably the most potent symbol of transformation. It is the heat of a roaring fire and the gentleness of a candle burning in the night. It is our hearth fires and our central heating; it provides us with what we need to cook our food. It is the sun that brings life and warmth to the land. We depend on fire for survival, but we also know fire's destructive powers. It is the distant stars in the night sky. It is volcanoes and the magma deep within the earth.

The cardinal direction of south is where we find the element of fire, the warrior at the height of their ability and maturity. It is passion and love, sex and pleasure. It is the power of manifesting; it is the doing, not the thinking. It is the time of the fiery noon-day sun at its nadir. The season is summer. Its colours are red and orange.

In spellcraft we work with fire in candle magic, burning items or petitions as well as working with the solar tides. Fire can be used for courage, protection, increasing energy, and strengthening will. Fire is power. We can make a needfire, which is a fire made from nine magical woods. We can scry in the flames of a candle or fire to gain insight into a situation. We can offer up herbs and incense to the gods, allowing the smoke to take our prayers to deity.

Fire is connected with the tarot suit of wands, but many see this element as connected to swords, being as the sword is forged in fire. We discussed the reason for the association with swords and the element of air in the previous element, air, where Waite (from the Rider-Waite-Smith tarot deck) switched the wands and swords associations in order to keep his vows of secrecy to the Golden Dawn. I personally prefer swords corresponding to fire, but if you work with the tarot you may prefer air.

Magical creatures associated with fire are dragons and salamanders. Lizards, snakes, scorpions, and other desert creatures are also associated with fire. The stag is also sometimes associated with the element of fire.

Herbal correspondences with the element of fire include alexanders, cedar, coriander, chili, cinnamon, clove, clover, dragon's blood, fennel, heather, holly, juniper, mandrake, mustard, nettle, rosemary, thyme, St. John's wort, and sunflower.

Water

Water is seen as feminine and rules the western quarter. It is the setting sun over the sea and the twilight of evening. It is middle to old age, the wisdom years gained from experience. It is rain and all bodies of water. It is nurturing and holding, yet still with an element of danger, as are all of the elements and they are to be respected. It is the cool and damp autumn after the harsh summer, and it is the golden years of our lives.

With the element of water we find love and peace, forgiveness and letting go. Just as the tides ebb and flow, so too do our emotions and the cycles of our lives. It is often the place of the otherworld in various cultures, travelled to by a journey over water. It is mystery and the quiet, mundane rest at the end of a long day. Beneath the waves are portals to the faery realm; across the water and through the mists are where the Lady of the Lake dwells. It is where the otherworld lies, beyond the ninth wave. Its colours are the blues and indigos of the sea and the twilight sky.

In spellcraft we work with water in various ways, often through scrying, a form of divination where we gaze into the water for images and clues. Water is often used in spellcraft for peace, healing, friendship, and purification. Items are often cast into bodies of water for various purposes; think wishing wells and the offerings our ancient ancestors made to lakes and rivers.

In the tarot, water is associated with the suit of cups. The iconic image of the cup is seen in many mythologies, most famously in the Arthurian Grail myths. But we also have older vessels, the cauldrons that we find in much of Celtic lore, such as the cauldron of Annwn or the cauldrons of Ceridwen or Dagda. These are all vessels of transformation, and within their dark depths we can drink of the elixir of life and the *awen* (inspiration) that reflects our journeys from our beginnings in the watery womb all the way to the tomb and beyond. The Grail is a symbol of sovereignty. It is also the shared vessel of friendship and trust, the drinking horn or vessel of Norse mythology, passed between the group, over which is spoken words that become sealed in fate. It is the stirrup cup at the start of the hunt; it is the "parting glass" of Scottish folklore drunk at the end of a gathering of friends.

> *In Witchcraft, the tools most associated with water are the chalice and the cauldron. The chalice is simply a smaller, more modern form of the cauldron. It is a tool that is sacred to the Goddess, and to drink from the chalice in ritual is to partake of her divine energy.*

Magical creatures associated with water are mermaids and merfolk of all kinds, undines, selkies, kelpies, and nereids. Other animals associated with the element of water include whales, dolphins, and fish of all kinds but especially the salmon in Celtic folklore. There is also the beaver, otter, frogs, herons and other waterfowl, and, of course, made famous in Witchcraft through Shakespeare, the newt, which is of the salamander genus (not the magical creatures) but is partially aquatic. (I have nine currently living in my pond. They moved in soon after we dug out the pond and filled it with water and aquatic plants.)

Herbal correspondences are comfrey, marshmallow, rushes, water lilies, apples (think the island of Avalon, the Isle of Apples), aloe, cucumber, daffodil and narcissus, datura, foxglove, hemlock, ivy, lettuce, willow, valerian, and seaweed of all kinds.

Aether (Spirit)

The fifth element is often termed as spirit or aether, and this element has all of the other elements contained within it. It is the highest vibration of all the elements and can be found in our auras, or energy/etheric fields that surround our bodies, as well as being in our bodies themselves; it is everything. It is sometimes referred to as the life force itself or deity or Source. It is all times and no time, all stages of life and none. It is all colours and all things.

Its power lends itself to everything. It is the loom upon which all manifestation is woven. It is the balance of all the other elements coming together in unity.

When we have the four elements working with each other in this perfect balance, the fifth element of aether or spirit appears. This is why we have a pentagram in the Craft, which shows the four elements plus spirit, which binds it all together. The elements in the pentagram below are placed according to the invoking and banishing ritual elements found in certain traditions. Some traditions may differ in their elemental associations, but this is perhaps the most popular.

DIAGRAM 2: *Pentagram and Elements*

Some within the Craft prefer to follow the Celtic method of seeing the world of manifestation and spirit through the perception of land, sea, and sky, with sacred fire at the heart. Awen, or inspiration, might be the connecting force that occurs when all realms are held in balance. How you choose to view the elements or the realms in your own work will depend upon your own preferences.

Adapting the Correspondences to Your Own Environment

The elements as they are presented here are probably the most well-known in Witchcraft and in modern Paganism. However, the attributes associated with them might not work for you in your own environment. You might not associate water with the direction of west or the season of autumn, for example. For me, growing up in Canada, the nearest ocean was to the east of me. West was the huge landmass of the country. The season in which we had the most water was spring, with the rains and the snow melt causing flooding, rushing rivers and bringing life back to the land.

While the attributes described in this chapter reflect more classical and traditional associations, remember that they were created within a context. That context might not work for you. Then again, you may choose to use it as it is known in this format because these associations have developed an energetic resonance from being used for many, many years. I have seen traditions use the classical model and traditions that create their own, and they all have been perfect to their purpose.

Where I live now in Suffolk, UK, on the coast of the North Sea, the classical view of the elements and their corresponding directions doesn't quite work. In the east there lies a vast body of water: the North Sea. The sun rises each morning over the cold, grey waters, so for me, water is in the east. To the south is fire, where the warm winds sometimes carry the red dust of the Sahara Desert to coat our homes and cars in a fine film and also provide glorious sunrises and sunsets due to the amount of particles in the air. To the west lies the landmass of England and Wales, and beyond that Ireland, so west is the element of earth for me. The north is where the icy cold winds come down from the Arctic, down through Norway, and hit our lands with their chill and cause temperatures to drop whatever the season, therefore north is associated with the element of air in my own Hedge Witchcraft tradition.

A good thing to do—daily if possible, but weekly is good enough—is to spend some time casting your awareness to each of the four directions to feel what is going on in your landscape. Feel which element is strongest in each direction and come to understand the associations that come with it in your local area. Simply sit silently, relax, and expand your awareness in a particular direction. It helps if you know what landmarks and features lie in each direction so you can cast your attention to these before expanding further. I can feel the sea in one direction and whether the water is quiet or stormy, the tides high or low. In another direction I can feel the bustle or quietude of the village. In another direction I can feel the ancestors and the ancient *tumuli*—henges and villages that no longer exist—right alongside the more modern farmers' fields. In yet another direction I can feel the expanse of the great forest and whether it is quiet and relaxed or busy with tourists and other folk.

I am casting the net of my awareness wider in each direction to inform me of what is happening in the landscape and also help me locate myself in the greater picture. This practice is extremely helpful if I want to be part of a crowd or avoid people or find high-energy places. I can use this practice to find where the deer are on the heath or if there is a hunting party nearby. I know when the beach will be quiet and when the car park will be full. I can use the elemental associations in each of the directions in my locality to add to my magical practices, develop my intuition, and generally grant me an awareness of my own surroundings. This is also an ability that I can take with me wherever I go in order to understand the elements and the locality in which I find myself at any given time.

We must learn to use all our senses and our own awareness, which is not just limited to our bodies. In Hedge Witchcraft we are so much more than our bodies, and we can expand our awareness further.

We have many stories of witches who did this in the past, sometimes flying through the air on their broomsticks or transforming into hares in order to walk about the land and find out information. This art is not something that can be lost if we do not let it be lost. It is there for anyone to rediscover and work with.

*S*he stands in the ritual circle and calls to the
elements to lend their aid to her spellwork on
this midsummer night. Facing the north, she stands
firm, palms facing outwards, and calls with honour
and respect the element of air. She whispers all the
associations that air has for her, and soon she feels
the element coming into her working. "Hail and welcome," she says, bowing to the direction. She moves
and does the same for the east, south, and west with
other ritual gestures, then stands in the centre of
her circle to call in spirit. Once she has attuned to
all the energies in perfect balance, she knows that
she stands at the centre of something very special,
a place where she can craft her spells with the aid
of the elements, her own knowledge and intuition,
the Fair Folk whom she has worked with for years,
and the Goddess and God themselves. For this brief
moment, she knows that all is within her; that all
is held in balance and working with each other. She
breathes in deeply and then gets to work.

8

The Fair Folk

We call them faerie.
We don't believe in them.
Our loss.

• • • • • •

Charles de Lint,
Moonlight & Vines

In this chapter, we'll look at the importance of the Fair Folk and the otherworld in relation to the Craft of the hedge witch. As one who walks between the worlds, knowledge of the history and lore is quite essential so that any working with the Fair Folk is done safely, respectfully, and honourably.

Who Are The Fair Folk?

Witches, healers, cunning folk, fairy doctors, and more have always had a good relationship with the Fair Folk, otherwise known as faeries. In fact, according to some historical accounts, these folks derived their powers from their association with the Fair Folk. But just who are the Fair Folk?

I use the term *Fair Folk* because it is traditional to not call faeries by their name and instead use friendly terms such as the Good Folk, the Good

Neighbours, the Gentry, the Shining Ones, and the Wee Folk, among others. Some also say that the Fair Folk find the term *faery* derogatory. Others have said that using the term brings their attention to you, which might not be the kind of attention you are seeking. There are many different types and names for the Fair Folk all over the world. In Britain there are so many different names for these beings: the Scottish Seelie (the Blessed) and Unseelie (Unblessed) courts, the Irish Sidhe (People of the Mounds) or Tuatha dé Danann (People of the goddess Danu), the Welsh Tylwyth Teg (the Fair Family) or the Bendith y Mamau (the Blessing of the Mothers), the Norse Alfar (light elves) and Svartalfar (dark elves), and the British brownies and kobolds, just to name a few.

Every region has its own kind of Fair Folk who dwell both in this world and the otherworld and who cross over and help or hinder humanity as they see fit. In my region of East Anglia, the Fair Folk are also known as Pharisees, Ferishers, Hikey Sprites, Frairies, and more. These otherworldly folk can travel between the worlds, which is probably why witches (and especially hedge witches) work with them regularly. To cross over into the otherworld or have contact with these beings can gain the seeker knowledge regarding the healing of animals, the properties of plants, and the charms needed to help people in their day-to-day lives. In this quest, this seeking of information, the witch demonstrates her courage and her wits, for you need both to work with the Fair Folk.

The relationship between humanity and the Fair Folk has been mixed in the stories we have had handed down throughout the centuries. Some would say that the Fair Folk are to be feared and are harmful to humanity. Others say that the Fair Folk are much like humans in that there are good and bad ones in any given bunch. Yet again others say that what you bring into an interaction with the Fair Folk is what you will get out of it, so if you go in with darkness in your heart, that is what you will get in return. Some of the stories of harmful encounters with the Fair Folk may indeed be Christian propaganda to encourage the rural folk to stop interacting with them. In my opinion, this is highly likely. I believe that as with any relationship with any being, you need to be fully aware, respectful, cautious, mindful, polite, and open. Do not seek to trick the Fair Folk, for things will go badly for you. Some say that the Fair Folk are the ones who love to trick, but I think that they are simply asking you to be intelligent in your choices, sometimes even making you do so, learning lessons along the way that will benefit you in future situations, both in this world and the otherworld.

In the Scottish witch trials of the Middle Ages, we see many accounts of those accused of Witchcraft consorting with the faeries, rather than the standard "consorting with the devil." This is interesting because it might demonstrate a cultural heritage of working with the Fair Folk that had already been forgotten in England and other countries. In the more remote areas such as Scotland and Ireland, Cornwall and Brittany, the lore and knowledge of the Fair Folk may indeed have survived longer.

The Irish have a tradition of fairy doctors, who use their relationship with the Fair Folk to heal and help those around them. Sometimes they were also called witches, though that term didn't quite have the baggage that it did in the rest of Europe at the time. That does not mean that it was easy for those who worked with the Fair Folk. The last witch to have been "burned" in Ireland (she was beaten by her husband and then stuffed into the fireplace) was Bridget Cleary, whose home was built on a fairy fort and who, one day, stopped off at another nearby fairy fort while doing her egg delivery rounds (she was rumoured to have an interest in the Fair Folk).[35] It's thought that Bridget knew herbal healing, like her mother, which gave her a power that made her husband wary of her.[36] Bridget fell ill after her visit to the nearby fairy fort, and her husband accused her of being a changeling. It's most likely that she caught a cold, which turned into pneumonia. Bridget's story is a sad one of domestic violence, abuse, and the misogyny and sexism that was becoming the norm in Ireland and around the world at the time due to the growing patriarchal influence of

35 Purcell, "Waterford Treasures."
36 Bourke, *The Burning of Bridget Cleary*, 67.

the church.[37] Indeed, all of the witch trials and abuses suffered can be seen in this light, with headstrong women (and some men) suffering the loss of their power to those who would take it for themselves.

One must be bold to seek out the Fair Folk. Even those who follow the Christian God may still feel the call to find them, to seek them out in their places. One such fellow was the Reverend Robert Kirk, a Scottish minister and folklorist who wrote the now-famous *Secret Commonwealth of Elves, Fauns and Fairies*. Kirk's work was never published in his lifetime, otherwise who knows what abuses he himself may have suffered because of it. At the time of writing, the Christian church was very much in power and the low esteem for the Old Ways was apparent. Even in the text, the disregard for women is seen in Kirk's writing, where he often states that women don't have the skill or the capabilities of the mind to see the Fair Folk like the men. Kirk collected accounts of fairy contact all throughout the Scottish Highlands, and it is said he had some encounters himself.

Kirk describes the faeries as thus:

> These *siths* or fairies they call *sluagh maithe* or the good people (it would seem, to prevent the dint of their ill attempts, for the Irish use to bless all they fear harm of) and are said to be of a middle nature between man and angel (as were daemons thought to be of old), of intelligent studious spirits, and light, changeable bodies (like those called astral) somewhat of the nature of a condensed cloud and best seen in twilight. These bodies be so pliable through the subtlety of the spirits that agitate them that they can make them appear or disappear at pleasure.[38]

Before his death, Kirk often walked around the local fairy hills, and after he had died, it was said that he had been taken by the Fair Folk. Scottish folklorist Stewart Sanderson said that Kirk "was in the habit of taking a turn in his nightgown on summer evenings on the fairy hill beside the manse, in order to get a breath of fresh air before retiring to bed: and one

---

37 Bourke, *The Burning of Bridget Cleary*, 58.
38 Kirk, *The Secret Commonwealth*.

evening in 1692, 14 May, his body was found lying, apparently dead, on the hill."[39] It was said that the Fairy Queen had taken a liking to Kirk, and he became her chaplain instead.

The many accounts of the bold and the unwitting having encounters with the Fair Folk have been passed down through time: "Thomas the Rhymer," "The Ballad of Tam Lin," and *A Midsummer Night's Dream* are among the hundreds of other tales (and fairy tales) that have been passed down through the centuries, through different cultural strands and religious/spiritual beliefs. There is sorrow and joy in many of them, and they all have something to teach the witch.

The Fair Folk are beings older than us humans; they have walked our lands and theirs for many, many eons before we even arrived on the scene. They are proud and ancient. We have many stories of their powers, such as teaching human folk/magic practitioners about their own ways of magic. They may also be less benevolent: abductors and seducers, leaving changelings in the place of human babies, and luring the unwary into their dark abodes with the beauty of their fairy glamour. They may also be vessels of sovereignty for ancient kings, working with humanity for the good of all. Their roles are vast and varied, and we simply cannot pin them down to one purpose or intention.

Perhaps the most important thing the Fair Folk can teach us is about our own land and its history and occupants, both the seen and the unseen. Witches (and many scientists, to a differing degree) know that there is more to the world than what can be seen with the naked eye. The places where we can meet with the Fair Folk are the local places of power in our landscape. These will vary from region to region and country to country. Here in Britain, it is often the mounds, barrows, or the ancient tumuli (burial sites) that are the doorways to the otherworld. Ancient structures such as the Neolithic mining pits here in East Anglia are also portals to the otherworld, as we can see in the story of the Green Children of Woolpit here in my home county of Suffolk. One day two "green children" were

39 Sanderson, "A Prospect of Fairyland."

found just outside the village of Woolpit. When asked where they came from, they pointed to the terrain pockmarked with what we now know as ancient mining pits but which were then known as "wolf pits." From these pits the children emerged from a subterranean land—St. Martin's Land, they called it, where the sun never shone but it was always twilight. The children were taken into the custody of a local lord, and they didn't eat anything offered to them until they were offered something green. The sister eventually began to eat different foods and thrived, though she was considered peculiar. The younger brother declined until he eventually passed away.

Then again, there are also the old fairy forts, which are often the remnants of Iron Age structures but sometimes are just rocky outcroppings out in the wilderness, lonely places where few humans go and at which the faeries gather. These places speak to us of our heritage and of the close connection that the otherworld has with the dead and with the wild. As our world lies close to the otherworld, crossing over in both life and death is entirely plausible. Perhaps the Fair Folk are even the custodians of the souls of the dead before they move on, either to another incarnation or wherever they choose/are destined to travel. Then again, the stories of the Fair Folk might simply be tales told to explain these phenomena out in the landscape and perhaps serve as warnings not to go to these "dangerous" places. For who knows what you may find there: personal freedom, a refuge from the daily grind, a place to think for yourself, an increase in personal power...all things which certain folk want to prevent you from achieving.

Some even say that the Fair Folk are the embodiment of the energy of the land and the visible "spirit of place" or the soul/essence of the trees, rocks, etc. Personally I think that these are separate entities, but that is just from my own experience. The Fair Folk may be stewards of these spirits but are not the spirits themselves. You may have different experiences that can tell you otherwise. What is important is to be bold and seek them out, however you think you may find them, but there are always guidelines to help you in your encounters with the Fair Folk. You will have to use your wit and wisdom to see which guidelines apply to you and which do not, for some may be true and others mere superstition. We will look at some of the guidelines later on in this chapter.

What Do the Fair Folk Look Like?

Just as there is no standard height, weight, hair or skin colour, etc., for humans, so it is with the Fair Folk. In fact, they are even more diverse than us humans and can range in size from fitting in your hand to giant folk. These beings live all over the world; every culture has some definition of them relevant to their land. Here in Britain, our fairy lore is influenced by Celtic, Norse, and Germanic lore, with a bit of French language and culture thrown in. We have the small sprites, piskies, and pixies; the larger gnomes, dwarves, and kobolds; human-sized sidhe, elves, faeries, pharisees, and even the larger trolls, giants, and Shining Ones, just to name a few.

While I use the term *Fair Folk*, not all of these beings appear as fair or beautiful. Some can look like natural phenomena, such as creatures that appear to be made up of sticks or creatures that have bark- or stonelike skin. Some may have wings, but most do not. Some appear human with an ethereal beauty that shines from within like the starlight. Others are shadowy creatures or beings of glimmering light. Some are dark and dour; others happy and light. There is no rule for the faery realms, which is fluid and ever changing, a reflection of their nature and the natural world around us all.

The most remarkable ones that I have seen have had human appearances. I once saw a woman in white on a pathway that led out of town. She seemed to be a guardian of sorts, and I nodded to her. Her form was translucent, and I could see through her. In fact, I saw her more with my mind and only a little with my eyes, but I knew she was there. I greeted her respectfully and continued on my way, allowing her to see the love in my heart for the land around me.

Another time a being appeared one Beltane night in my back garden. My friends and I had finished a ritual, and after they had left I went to place the offering at the bottom of the garden. I was walking back to the house in a patch of moonlight and felt a presence behind me. I turned around and saw a shadowy form of a male figure standing about shoulder height and dressed in brown in front of the bird feeder. He was watching me. I shifted my gaze to see if there were others, and he disappeared.

I have also seen the Fair Folk in animal form. A white doe appeared on the heathland one spring, and she was beautiful to behold. Her other-worldliness literally shone through her, and she always seemed to shimmer in whatever light I beheld her, whether it was sunlight or an overcast day. She was different than the other deer in the herd. The first time I saw her, she approached to get a closer look at me. We stood looking at each other for a time, and then some people with their dog came near and she moved away. I have seen her many times since; she leads the herd of deer. They seem to follow her command. In Irish lore it is said that the deer are the "fairy cattle." Whenever I see her, she is watching me, looking at me as if she can see into my soul. I know that I have much to learn from her and much work to be done with her. I am very much looking forward to it.

The Fair Folk might appear as birds or any beast. Here in Suffolk we have the tales of Black Shuck, a huge black dog that wanders the heath-lands. It is said that if you see Black Shuck approaching you head-on, you will come to grief soon. If Black Shuck is walking parallel to you, he is offering you protection. I have not met him yet on my wanderings, but I felt quite a terrifying presence on the heath just after sunset one time near Samhain. The goats that were on this part of the heath were running away from something, which was odd, as they are accustomed to people and their dogs. The hairs stood out on the back of my neck, and I knew that I had to get out of there right away. The sun had gone down, the gate that led to the car park was two minutes away, and I ran for it. Once through the gate, I knew that I was safe.

There are trooping faeries, Fair Folk that go about the lands in groups. I have seen the very edge of this phenomenon once. I had been standing outside honouring the full moon. I was sitting at my picnic table, which overlooks the back garden. Suddenly my ears began to pop, and I felt a pressure inside my head. It seemed as if the air grew thick around me. I looked down to the bottom of the garden, where on the other side of the hedge lies a dirt track that runs the length of all the back gardens of the houses on this street, following a stream and down to an open area. Behind the hedge I could see the track suddenly light up with a silvery-blue glow, like the moonlight, only much stronger. I could hear bells and faint music, not with my ears but with my mind, and I knew that I shouldn't be there: this was a time for the Fair Folk. My heart began to race, and much as I wanted to see more, I knew that this was not for my eyes. The Fair Folk value their privacy as much as we do, so I returned inside. As soon as I entered the house, the sounds stopped and the pressure in my head eased. I looked out the window; I couldn't help myself. All was normal, though I knew that the veil between the worlds had thinned and that they had passed on their Faery Rade, the procession of Fair Folk that traverses the land along roads of power, or fairy roads.

I have also felt this power one night as I was driving home along the heath after teaching a dance class. Again, it was around Samhain. Just before the village boundary, I pulled the car into a layby and stood outside to feel the winds upon my face. The clouds were scudding across a dark sky, and the orange lights from the nearby port gave the sky an otherworldly appearance. I stood there for a minute and then felt a dread coming upon me. The wind whipped and howled, and then I heard *The Wild Hunt rides* in my mind. I immediately heeded that warning, got back into the car, and drove home. You just don't take chances on lonely, windswept nights like these.

There are Fair Folk who live in different locations, from the forest to the sea, the lakes and the mountains, above and below ground. There are the Irish water horses who lie in wait along bodies of water to catch the unwary and drown them. There are the woodwoses and woodwives who tempt the unwary in the dark forests. Mermaids and mermen abound along the coastline of Britain, and we even have the tale of the Wild Man of Orford, a merman who was caught in the river leading out to the sea here in Suffolk.

Some of the Fair Folk might even live in your house. Brownies and kob-olds are said to live with families, providing aid in return for offerings of food and drink (but never offer them clothing; according to the folklore, it offends them and will drive them away). You might even find certain parts of your garden seem to have an in-dwelling spirit that relates to the Fair Folk. The Fair Folk live alongside humanity, and their many interactions with us in folklore attest to their presence here.

They are able to traverse between the worlds, which is why we, as hedge witches, are often drawn to them. We share in that wanderlust, the thirst to know more about the world around us, both the seen and the unseen. We also know that we can move between the worlds, and we can enter their realm just as they can enter ours. We have much to learn from each other about how to care for ourselves and our worlds.

Guidelines for Meeting the Fair Folk

It is important to note that I use the term *guidelines*, for these are not hard-and-fast rules that are set in stone. The way you can interact with those from the otherworld will vary from person to person, situation to situation, and place to place.

Here are some of the most well-known for the witch.

BE POLITE. No one likes to be treated rudely. Treat the Fair Folk with respect.

FIND OUT WHAT KIND OF OFFERINGS THEY ENJOY. This will vary from region to region, and you may find hints in your local folklore. Then again, asking the Fair Folk also helps! Giving an offering is a sign of friendship. It is not a bribe. You cannot bribe the Fair Folk.

BE CAREFUL WHAT YOU SAY. I have read in some lore that you never should say "thank you" to the Fair Folk because it puts you in their debt; others say that it is dismissive. While I used to adhere to this rule, I no longer do, for the Fair Folk that I work with don't mind it a bit. In fact, I always felt bad for not saying thank you, but they understood. I've never used a "thank you" in a dismissive or condescending tone, and I have indeed been thankful for their help, and I meant it. Mean what you say and say what you mean in all encounters, not just with the Fair Folk. You might find people do the same for you.

RESPECT WHERE THEY LIVE. If you muck about with their favourite places, you will suffer. This also applies to their fairy roads and pathways, the paths of energy that they use to travel from one place to another.

DON'T STARE. I think this falls into the "be polite" category, but sometimes you can get so caught up that you forget. No one likes to be stared at, so just remember this guideline should you seek them out and find them or should your paths happen to cross. If they appear, you will know whether you should be there or not, for you will either get a feeling of welcome, indifference, or dread. If you feel dread, move away quickly. This is not a time for humans.

DON'T EAT OR DRINK ANYTHING THEY OFFER YOU. This one is tricky because in some tales it's a lot worse to decline a gift from the Fair Folk, whether it's food or drink or a gift in some other form. You'll have to decide for yourself, and it may be entirely dependent upon the situation, which could vary from being to being and encounter to encounter. Similarly, the Fair Folk love to dance, and some say that if you dance with them, you will dance until you drop dead. Again, this may be an influence or idea from a rival religion seeking to stop interaction with the Fair Folk. I have heard folk tell of accepting a drink from the Fair Folk and not suffering any ill consequences. In fact, they felt that to refuse would have been the wrong thing to do.

Take Special Care During Their Powerful Celebration Days and Nights, Such As Beltane, Midsummer, and Samhain. The veils between the worlds are thin at these times, and you may unknowingly cross over or have interactions with them unprepared. Be aware of these times, be aware of yourself and your surroundings, and then you will be able to meet and work with them with intention.

Use Your Wits and Intelligence, and Protect Yourself Should You Feel the Need to Do So. This applies to any interaction, whether it is human, animal, plant, or otherworldly. Know who it is you wish to contact and how to do it. Do your homework. If you feel you need a little protection, you can also research that. Charms, herbs, and other protections abound in this area, but remember they may also hinder your encounter. The best protection is to keep your wits about you and know what you are doing; be brave but not foolhardy.

They Don't Like Iron. Again, there is debate here as some stories tell us that the Fair Folk can't abide the sight or presence of iron, while in other stories the Fair Folk are some of the very best smiths and work with iron, forging magical swords and other weapons and bestowing them upon humans. You will have to research the lore of your area to find out for yourself.

Time Runs Differently in the Otherworld. You might think you've been gone a few minutes, only to find out that an hour or longer has passed. Keep your wits about you.

How to Meet with the Fair Folk

The best places to meet with the Fair Folk are the liminal places. As both you and they can cross between the worlds, it makes sense to do this in places where the veil is thin. These are the in-between places, such as at the shore of a lake or the sea, where the land meets the water, or a mountain or hilltop, where the earth meets the sky. It might be a wild and lonely place, such as an ancient stone circle on a windy moor or the open heathland with the evening's mist creeping in. It could even be a space that you create to be a place between the worlds, such as a magic circle that is cast for that very purpose (more on circle casting later). You might also meet the Fair Folk at ancient mounds and fairy forts, burial mounds, dolmens, stone circles, and ringforts, should those be in your local landscape. Wherever you wish to seek out the Fair Folk, go prepared, not only to meet with them, but also in a practical sense: wear appropriate clothing, tell someone where you've gone or leave a note, and take all necessary precautions both when travelling and at your destination.

There are also liminal times that you can use, such as dawn and dusk, which are neither day nor night. You can use the witching hour of midnight, when one day turns over to the next (according to our modern clock/timekeeping). You could meet with them at the first signs of a new season, such as when the first spring flowers appear or when the first frost covers the land. There are also traditional times said to be when the Fair Folk are out and about the most, such as the three fairy nights of Beltane, Midsummer, and Samhain. Then again, you might come across them at any time, day or night, in any place!

The more open you are to meet with the Fair Folk, the more likely you are to have an encounter with them. Being a Doubting Thomas will most likely not yield a very good result, though sometimes the Fair Folk might just want to have a laugh and see the look on your face when you do come across them.

Working as a hedge witch, you will come across those from the otherworld. It is therefore imperative to research all that you can from the history and folklore of your area so that you are best prepared for these encounters. One of the best guides you can find on British fairy folklore is *Explore Fairy Traditions* by Jeremy Harte. You must also use your wits and courage to seek them out through modern means and with the ancient knowledge held deep in your heart.

For the Fair Folk are not beings stuck in time,
belonging only to Ye Olde Worlde. They are
right here, right now, living and working
alongside us, watching us develop and grow.

We will look at rites and rituals to work with the Fair Folk in chapter 13.

*T*here was a sense of unrest in the wood. She hadn't felt it
because she hadn't been open to it, being too preoccupied
with her own thoughts, but now they called out to her with
force. She looked up and it seemed like a tree was falling down
on top of her. She sucked in her breath, dived to the side, and
then looked back. All was as it was before. It was a warning
that something wasn't right. Shaken, she knew that she must
investigate. She asked the Fair Folk where she should look. She
felt a strong pull towards an old hollow tree that had seven
trunks growing out of it—the Seven Sisters. The hedge witch
made her way to the tree and instantly knew what was wrong.

Surrounded by a ring of sawdust, the Seven Sisters Fairy
Tree had been cut down. Despair filled her heart. She lay her
hand on the trunk and knew why she had been attacked earlier. She poured her love out for the tree and for the wood,
her grief blending with that of her surroundings. Together
they keened into the late afternoon light. When they were
done, she reached into her bag and drew a flask of mead. She
sprinkled the mead around the remaining trunk, whisper-
ing prayers for the wood and for the Fair Folk. Many were
the times when she had peered through the hole in the trunk
to see the other side. Figures of the Fair Folk, shimmering
and light, wandered amidst the beech wood in the distance.
She knew that they would not come to this place anymore,
but still she needed to help heal the wound that had been
inflicted upon the site. She felt their presence around her in
this place one final time as she and the Fair Folk whispered
their farewells to the Seven Sisters.

PART 3
Ritual & the Art of Hedge Riding

In this section, we will look at the elements contained within the practice of hedge riding and how to perform it and other works of the Craft in ritual.

9

Hedge Riding

Between two worlds life hovers like a star,
'Twixt night and morn,
upon the horizon's verge.
How little we know that which we are!

• • • • • •

Lord Byron,
"Don Juan," Canto XVI

Hedges have so many uses. They mark boundaries, they protect, they shelter, they can provide food, and they can also be used to travel between the worlds. In this chapter, we'll look at the art of hedge riding and how it can be used by the hedge witch to travel between the worlds.

What Is Hedge Riding?

Hedge riding is at the heart of the practice of the hedge witch. It is the art of travelling between this world and the otherworld. It is closely linked to the witch and her Craft. The Germanic word *haeg* means both "hedge" and "hag," so we can see linguistically just how interlinked these two concepts are.

We all know the image of the witch sitting astride her broom. But do we know why she is doing that? Is it because she is flying through the night sky, cackling with freedom and fun? Maybe; it does sound like a great time. But really, in Hedge Witchcraft it is generally accepted that the witch is riding the world tree in order to access the otherworld. In the otherworld she can find what she needs to progress in her work here in this world. She can call upon the aid of the Fair Folk and otherworldly allies to help her in her Craft.

In some druid traditions, the world tree is used in a shamanic sense in order to journey through both this world and the otherworld. The otherworld is known to have three parts: the lowerworld, middleworld, and upperworld. It is in these realms that the druid can quest the awen, or seek inspiration or insight into a matter, gain guidance from otherworldly beings, ancestors, or even the divine. The hedge can be considered similar to the world tree in that it separates the worlds and is the access point upon which we can gain information, wisdom, and experience from the otherworld.

It wasn't only the druids who knew how to travel between the worlds using a tree motif. Hedge riding is an ancient art, with forms seen across the globe. For example, we see that it was used by the Norse as recorded in the *Hávamál*, a poem that contains the wisdom and sayings of Odin. In it, it states:

> *I know this the tenth:*
> *If I see the hedge-riders magically flying high,*
> *I can make it so they go astray*
> *Of their own skins, and of their own souls.*[40]

Don't let this quote put you off hedge riding or give you any fear. Hedge riding is safe, as you are working with both the conscious and subconscious mind at the same time. However, you might want to make a mental note not to tick off Odin...

In this book, we will be using hedge riding in a different and more specific way. We will be using the liminal places, times, and energies while

---

40 Pennick, *Runic Lore and Legend.*

hedge riding to travel to the otherworld, meet with the Fair Folk, and learn from them what it is that we need for our work. We will establish friends and connections in the realms of the Fair Folk and use various techniques to take us there in our hedge-riding practice. Much as the witches of the past worked with the Fair Folk, so too will we focus our hedge-riding practice on our connection with them and their land. The emphasis is very heavily placed on working with the realms of Faery in the otherworld, gaining knowledge and inspiration and using it here, in this world, for the betterment of all. In my previous book we focused on Celtic forms of the Fair Folk; however, in your Hedge Witchcraft you can focus on the Fair Folk of your own region, wherever you are in the world.

Witches and Brooms
Sex Magic, Sexual Fantasy, or Something Far Greater?

You might occasionally come across this topic in your hedge-riding research. Usually someone will gleefully tell you how witches got their kicks with their broomsticks. Over the years during my research on the history and roots of Witchcraft, I've heard quite a few people equate the riding of the broom by a witch to a sexual experience. Often these folks state that the witch used a hallucinogenic ointment that was rubbed onto the broom and then inserted in a sexual manner, which made her think she was "flying." I can tell you there are a lot easier ways to get high and get off.

This theory comes from a few confessions extracted during the dreadful times of the witch hunts across Europe. What is often forgotten or purposefully left out is the fact that these so-called confessions were extracted under torture. Europe and Scotland had absolutely awful methods of torturing so-called witches to extract information from them, usually with questions led by the examiner to produce a consistent result among the captives. In England torture was illegal; however, they still kept their victims awake and used sleep deprivation to get what they wanted, as well as having the person kept in one position for hours at a time without being able to move. That's torture too.

If we are to believe that what was said under torture is factually correct, then we must also believe what else was said alongside these so-called confessions. We must believe that these people had sexual congress with goats or the devil. We must believe that these people suckled their familiars (animal helpers) with their own blood. We must believe a host of other outrageous stories that were created to instil fear and hatred, dividing a populace and creating a space where the old, the weak, the poor, and the independent thinkers were targeted against the power of the church and patriarchy.

It is my firm belief that the sexual imagery of the witch "riding" her broom is the result of the sexually repressed minds of the witch hunters themselves. It is only one of many sexual fantasies created by these men who were paid to bring people in for prosecution. This was their job, and they made money from it. You would have to be quite a horrible type of person to want to do this sort of job in the first place.

In fact, the witch riding her broom comes from a long heritage of witches working with staffs, stangs, wands, and distaffs. We can trace this work in Europe back to the *völva* (plural *völur*), a type of Norse shamanistic practitioner of magic and divination. *Völva* actually means "staff carrier." Usually a female practitioner, she always had a staff, sometimes wood, sometimes an ornamental iron distaff. We know this from the many burials found across Scandinavia that have these women buried with the tools of their trade. We also have depictions of them in the literature, such as the *Völuspá* and the *Saga of Erik the Red.*

You might also occasionally hear someone say that the practice of the völva was seen as shameful in Viking society. They use the sexual fantasy imagery and overlay it against the profession of the völva, claiming that this is what she did with her staff, like a witch riding her broom covered in the flying ointment. This is wrong on many levels. First, let's address the "shameful" aspect.

For women, it was not considered shameful to practice magic, except from a Christian point of view. For men to practice the magic of the völva, known as seidr, it was seen in Viking times as *ergi*, often translated as "shameful." For a man to do women's work was seen as unmanly, though we do have to remember that the sources from which we get this information were written after the Viking period by the patriarchal Christian monks. In the archaeology we also see women warriors buried with their weapons, so the question of men's work and women's work is even more circumspect. Then we get into the myths of the gods and goddesses, where we see a few of the gods doing womanly things: Odin learns the art of seidr from the goddess Freya (he's not seen as unmanly), Thor dresses up as a woman to get into a giant's hall (still not unmanly), and Loki turns himself into a mare to have sex with another horse (*still* not called out as unmanly and actually producing Odin's steed, Sleipnir, in the process).

Add on top of that the fact that all the burials found of the women who are considered to be völur are high-status burials, and the question of shame seems absurd. The Osberg ship burial, perhaps one of the most famous Viking ship burials, had the body of a völva laid to rest with a host of beautiful treasures. No person who was considered shameful would be given such a send-off.

The question of drugs does come into play when looking at the ancestors of the more modern-day version of the broom-riding witch. Many of the burials were found to have pouches of hallucinogenic herbs on the body, such as henbane or cannabis seeds. When thrown onto hot coals, these seeds would produce a smoke that, when inhaled, would probably get you high, but not in the way that the sexual fantasy of the witch riding a broomstick would by the witch hunters. The clue is in the staff itself and what it symbolises. And no, it's not phallic in nature.

The word *seidr* is thought to derive from "spinning" or "weaving." The völur were those who could see the way that fate was woven or spun through their contact with the spirit world. Their distaffs were their link to that ability. For those graves wherein a wooden staff was found, the link lies more with the world tree that one can use to travel to the nine worlds in Norse cosmology. Through the staff there is a sympathetic link created with the world tree, with Yggdrasil, and it can be used to "ride" between the worlds. You either spun your connection to the otherworld or you rode the world tree.

And this is where the descendants of the völur appear today in the form of hedge riding as an aspect of Hedge Witchcraft. Riding the staff/stang/broom/whatever you have to hand that resembles the world tree helps you travel between the worlds in order to find the information that you require in your Craft. Most hedge witches today do not use hallucinogens, being able to perform the working through trance states that are induced by other means.

So, in conclusion, the equating of broom riding and sex seems more like a far-fetched fantasy than the actual reality when we dig a little deeper into the history and ancestry of Witchcraft. That it is continuing to be spread today only helps to demean and undermine the power of women in working magic, turning something extremely symbolic and important into a sexually repressed fantasy created by the patriarchy.

When a witch is riding her broom or using
her staff, stang, or wand in ritual, the lineage
is far greater than most people can ever
assume—and it is far more powerful than
any witch hunter could ever dream of.

What Happens in Hedge Riding?

Many people have different interpretations of what happens during the process of hedge riding. For the most part, it is seen as a form of astral travel, where we can leave our bodies behind and travel to the otherworld in spirit. That being said, I have travelled to the otherworld and come across beings there while fully in my body as I was out and about physically walking the land. I used liminal thresholds to determine the point at which I crossed over, and everything that I experienced physically happened in that in-between place—in a place that was between the worlds, neither fully in one nor the other but in a hazy, overlapping way of ever-changing fluidity.

When hedge riding, we are entering into a light trance in order to see the veils between the worlds so that we can move through them. This is best done when the conscious mind takes a bit of a back seat and we are able to allow our inner eyes and mind to work alongside the conscious mind. We are totally in control of our bodies and minds at all times as we learn to straddle the worlds and the areas of consciousness. We can allow both the conscious and the subconscious mind to inform us at the same time, working together to provide a broader view. In this way we are in control of ourselves and our situation. You can, of course, release the conscious mind completely should you so wish, but just be warned that in doing so, you are also releasing control. That is the reason that I do not use drugs or chemicals of any form in my hedge-riding practice.

I prefer to work with the in-between state of both conscious and subconscious, for it isn't an either/or situation here: we are fully capable of working with both at the same time.

This might be new to some people, who have been taught that it's either one or the other, but here in our Hedge Witchcraft, we know that there never is an either/or but rather a both/and mentality when it comes to perspectives and situations.

We can achieve this light trance state through drumming or movement such as rocking back and forth while seated. You can dance or even "tread the mill," a traditional Witchcraft practice that uses movement and an object as a focal point to create the trance-like effect (we will look at treading the mill in chapter 12). To cross over between the worlds, you can use chants or songs or even just through simply focusing your will on achieving this state. You can journey through meditation or even find the physical places where the worlds meet and cross over by simply stepping across or through a threshold. I will acknowledge that some days it is easier to achieve this state of mind than it is on other days, as our everyday lives do affect us physically, mentally, and spiritually.

I'll use an example of a physical walking between the worlds. I went out onto the heath with the intention of going out and drumming to the energy of the land and celebrating the springtide energies that were flowing through the landscape. When I got to the heathland where I like to work, I came across a portal to the otherworld that for some reason I had never noticed before. It was an old pine tree that had two trunks growing from the same base. I could clearly see that this was a portal to the otherworld, so I decided that as it had presented itself to me, I might as well go through and do my work on the other side too. I climbed up and through the portal and came out the other side. The air felt warmer and the rain was lighter, then stopped altogether. The light is always different in the otherworld, softer and more like the light shining through water. I went to my special place on the heath and danced and drummed and sang my joy, performing my ritual in both this world and the otherworld. I think the Fair Folk were pleased, as I felt my heart easing and was lighter of spirit at the end of it. Coming out of the heath, I usually pass by a threshold of hawthorn bushes, and I knew that once I crossed this, I would be fully back in my world again. And so I did, and immediately the sounds and sights of humanity crept back in, the light changed, and that sense of freedom faded a little.

I can also walk between the worlds with my walking stick in a meditation or through inner journeys. My walking stick represents the world tree, and by sitting cross-legged, holding my stick upright before me, I instantly feel able to travel between the worlds. The area around my third eye starts to buzz, and I sink into a trance in which it is so simple to move between the worlds. I can stand up and leave my body behind, flying out through the window in falcon form or walking out through the front door into a misty, hazy world and then out through the other side into the realm of the otherworld. There I can meet with friends and allies, places of power, and find what I need to bring back into my world. When I have finished my work, I simply return to my body through the window or back through the misty portal by my front door and re-enter my body. This form of hedge riding is simply done through the quiet and stillness of journeying and trance meditation.

There are examples of hedge riding from cultures all over the world. As we have seen, the Norse tradition of seidr was practised by a female practitioner of the arts known as a völva, who sat on a "high seat." This high seat represented the world tree and the practice of hedge riding. It was a wooden platform created to raise the völva and her consciousness. The völva also had a magic staff, another representation of the world tree, to help her on both her physical and her spiritual journeys (though sometimes this was an iron distaff, which was used more for weaving the magic than riding). She had women sing her into a trance, and there she performed divination, giving guidance from the spirits, the ancestors, and the gods to the people, much like oracular traditions the world over. Here in East Anglia there is a famous story of a witch who climbed a high platform in the fens to practice her magic against her foes—obviously a relic of this land's Scandinavian and European ancestors and their culture.

In this work we can use a particular tool as a representation of the world tree in order to do our hedge riding. This is the stang, a type of staff that is forked into two branches at the top.

The Stang/Stick/Wand

The stang is a staff that is forked at the top with two prongs. It symbolises the two worlds meeting together, the God and the Goddess, and all polarities. The stang is perhaps the tool *par excellence* of the hedge witch. You can, of course, use a broom; however, nowadays the stang is preferred, especially if you are going out of the house to do your work. It is the tool that can take you to the otherworld, serve as a focus for your travels, and also bring you back, having been made/found in this world. It is also a tool of protection, for staffs and sticks of all kinds have been used for millennia not only to aid a traveller in their journey by keeping their footing nice and steady, but also to ward off any who would wish them harm. The stang/stick/wand can be your safety, taking you out of any situation that you don't wish to be in and bringing you back to your world. Note, however, that sometimes uncomfortable situations are necessary for progress in your life's journey.

If you can't find a stang, an ordinary staff or walking stick will suffice until you are able or should you wish to find your own stang. I have used a simple hazel walking stick, the type that you can ride on the bus with or hike through the landscape, walk through town, or take into the shops without anyone looking twice. I also have a stang, which I use in private ritual only. Being much more conspicuous than my hazel walking stick, the larger stang would garner looks from folks. I use the stang for rites in my back garden or when I'm out on the lonely windswept beach. You can find smaller stangs that are the height of walking sticks with a smaller forked top, normally used in the past for walkers or shepherds in which the thumb is placed in between the fork for extra grip. These are called, funnily enough, thumbsticks. You can sometimes find these types of walking sticks in antique shops or at local country fairs where the crafting of them is still known. Occasionally they will have a pronged bit of stag antler instead of the usual wooden prong at the top. If you can't find your own stang or thumbstick, make your own! Again, these are less conspicuous than the tall stang; it really depends on where and how you want to work. All will work equally well.

If you absolutely cannot even have a walking stick, then you can always use a wand. This is simply a smaller version of the stang/stick and is much more portable. This might be a good substitute for those who live in cities. Wands are very easy to make, and you can easily hide them away in a bag.

If you are going to make your own stang/stick/wand, then you will have to research the type of tree you want to use. What are its magical properties? What are its physical properties? Both will be relevant in your work. In traditional Witchcraft the ash is often used; however, you may not have this type of tree in your local area. I have a birch wand made from a branch of a tree in my back garden that needed pruning. I found my stang on the heath in a wooded area where a birch tree had recently fallen. If you are using fallen wood, ensure that it has recently fallen. Old wood can be rotten inside, making it brittle and unusable. Birch trees are plentiful in my area; ash trees, much less so. My hazel walking stick was made for me as a gift by a park ranger.

If you are cutting a branch from a tree, ensure that you cut as close to the trunk as you can, as that will allow the wound to heal over quickly. Cut with a very sharp knife or saw, depending on the size of the branch. Always ask permission from the tree first, and leave an offering such as water, milk, or honey at the tree's base. If the tree doesn't give its permission, find another one. Walk around the tree clockwise three times, singing a song of thanks and beauty to the tree, if you are able, or simply speaking to it either out loud or in your mind. You will hear an answer in your mind or have a feeling that it is permitting you or denying you the branch you seek. If the tree doesn't reply, move on and find another tree.

Once you have your branch, take it home and strip off the bark if you wish to have a smooth surface. My hazel walking stick has the bark still left on, as it's very tight and smooth as it is. I stripped the flaky bark off my birch wand to reveal the lovely light wood beneath. Let the tool dry out for a few weeks, and then add a beeswax or linseed varnish, if you like. This will help the longevity of the tool. You can then add fabric or leather strips for the gripping area, tie a feather to it, or, in the case of a wand, add a crystal or stone tip to it should you so desire. Please ensure that the crystal tip is from the land where you live, preferably one that you found yourself. Crystal mining can be very destructive to a landscape, and you want to make sure that what you use is ethical. Living by the North Sea, we can often find belemnites, pointed bullet-shaped stones that are actually the fossilised remains of prehistoric squid-like beings. In folkore they are called "thunderbolts" or even "devil's bullets." They are the perfect shape for wand tips, especially if you have a wood that can be easily hollowed out: simply slide these lovely stones in until they're nice and tight!

Working with a Tree

Much like when I used the pine tree's natural threshold to cross over, so too are many trees associated with the otherworld. Any tree that is hollow is often thought to be a portal to the otherworld. If you can walk through the hollow, like some of the giant redwoods on the west coast of North America, you have a great portal right there!

Hedges, of course, are probably the most used trees in hedge riding, funnily enough. But why hedges? Well, hedges mark the boundary between one area and another. As such, they sit between the areas, or between the worlds. They are liminal places. The hole in the hedge at the bottom of my garden is very much a magical place, where all sorts of creatures—from badgers and deer to the Fair Folk—often come through. If you have a hedge on your property, see if you can work with it; befriend it and ask it to work with you on your journeys.

In times past it was the hedge that separated the civilised from the wild. It was a barrier that kept the wilderness out, the forest at bay. It also kept the livestock safe in an enclosed area, as hedges of blackthorn and hawthorn were often used (and are still used today) in areas where stone walls aren't possible (like here in East Anglia, where we have few stones apart from the pebbles and shingle on our beaches). There are some lovely ancient hedgerows still to be found in the British landscape, and these can be wonderful places to work (with the landowner's permission, if you are not on a public right of way/footpath). But your own back garden hedge can be a wonderful tool that you can use for your hedge riding. Sit in front or within it, if you can, and perform your meditative journeys there. Or visualise yourself standing before your hedge and taking a running leap over it and into the otherworld!

• • •

Later on in this work, we will look at rites and rituals to cross between the worlds. In the meantime, see if you can find a tree or hedge that you can work with or make your own stang/stick/wand. The point is to use something as a focus for the hedge or the world tree in your work, in order for you to travel between the worlds. If you are unable to have any tools, or even to access a tree or hedge, then you can always use the world tree in your mind.

Meditation on the World Tree

Sit in a comfortable position, either on the floor or in a chair. Settle your mind and take a few deep breaths. Close your eyes and see a misty space before you. The mists are shifting, slowly winding around and before you. They begin to dissolve and there you see the world tree. It stands tall and proud before you. Take note of the type of tree that it is, if you can discern this. Walk around it in your mind, looking at it from all angles. When you are familiar with the tree, ask it to show you how you can work with it. You might find a crack or doorway appears in the trunk through which you can travel to the otherworld. Or you might find a staircase that winds upwards into the branches or down into the roots where you can move between the worlds. You might simply be able to place a hand on the trunk and then move into the tree itself, sending your body like a mote of light to where it needs to go. Know that wherever you journey, you will be able to find the world tree whenever you need it, to get back to where you need to be. For now, however, simply note the tree and how it is offering you a method of journeying. We will later take you through some journeys to help you start on your hedge-riding path. Give your thanks to the world tree, then come back through the mists to where you are seated in this world. Take a few breaths, move slightly, and take time to fully return to yourself. Smile and give thanks.

• • •

Hedge riding is a wonderfully freeing and informative experience. You will gain personal insights and wisdom, as well as the wisdom and lore that you will learn from the Fair Folk. The art of hedge riding has so many uses, and, I'm sure, some that you will come up with solely on your own!

*S*he carves out the shape of a witch riding her broom across the moon on her jack-o'-lantern. As she does so, she smiles at the symbology of the image, which so few people know today. Here is the empowered practitioner of the arts travelling between the worlds, riding a version of the world tree that can be hidden in plain sight. For the arts of the witch were that of the country folk, and the tools they used were what they had at hand. This resonates with the hedge witch, and she steps back to look upon her work, a candle now lit within. She laughs out loud, a high, free cackle of delight, much like one would expect of the witch she carved into the pumpkin. Her soul is free and unfettered, and at any moment she too may grab her broom and be out riding the skies...

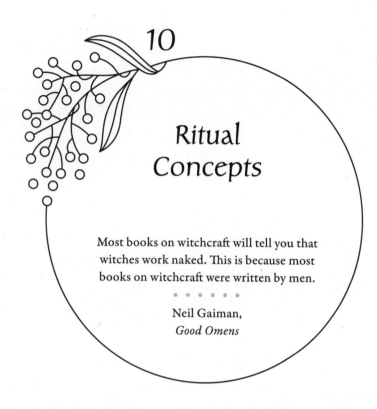

10

Ritual
Concepts

Most books on witchcraft will tell you that
witches work naked. This is because most
books on witchcraft were written by men.

• • • • • •

Neil Gaiman,
Good Omens

What is ritual? Why do we do rituals in Witchcraft? What is the purpose
and expected result in these kinds of workings? Here we will take a look at
these ideas as well as the basic elements of ritual so that you can create your
own. What follows here is not dogma; it is not something that is to be slav-
ishly followed, for it is not set in stone. What I present here is simply what
I have learned over my many, many years in the Craft. How you practice
your own Craft and tradition will be different, as it will be unique to you
and your own locale, preferences, style, and desires. The concepts below
are probably the most popular in many different traditions of Witchcraft,
including Hedge Witchcraft, so they will provide you with a good foundation to work with as you develop your own practice. Hedge riding is a
ritual act that is best performed with a solid foundation, so here we will
look at how to conduct a ritual, including the casting of a circle.

What Is a Ritual?

A ritual is simply an action that is repeated over and over again to achieve a specific result. It has been done repeatedly because it has been proven successful. We all have rituals in our daily lives, from the smallest rituals to the grandest. Our morning routine is a ritual: what we do as soon as we get out of bed, how we perform our daily ablutions. Cooking is another ritual: we often have very specific ways of doing things to get the desired result. The big rituals are, of course, those related to the big things in life, such as marriage or death. These all come with their own rituals, each different depending on the culture and the people engaging with them. If we don't perform a ritual, either in a large or small context, often we will feel out of sorts or that something is missing or incomplete. Rituals help us give structure to the ethereal moments; they provide us with a context in which we can understand the world and make some sense of it.

Why Do Ritual?

The structure that comes from ritual often offers us a pleasing sense of satisfaction. It provides us with a solid point in time in which something is done or acknowledged. It gives us a foundation to work with and develop other things upon, such as the rest of our day or the rest of our marriage or how we interact with deity, the ancestors, and the Fair Folk. Even though it can take us into the highest points of ecstasy, ritual is a very grounding thing, for ritual in Witchcraft is all about communion—with each other, with the divine, with the earth, and with nature. It is about dropping the boundaries and becoming part of everything that is happening right now. As musician Tori Amos once said, "If you don't become a part, you become apart in a horrible, scary way."[41] Ritual helps us to see where we fit into the grand scheme of things and how we can contribute to the world around us.

There are many reasons to perform ritual in Witchcraft. Probably the most important is to honour what is happening in nature all around us.

---

41   From a German television interview: https://youtu.be/s74xHTsqv30 (accessed 9 April 2021).

The sabbats and esbats help us identify with the time and place in which we stand, as well as acknowledge the beauty and gifts that come with that time, the lessons we can learn, and how we are a part of that cycle. These rituals remind us that deity is immanent and that what we see in the outer is also part of the inner.

Ritual is also performed to influence a certain outcome. We might work our spellcraft with a ritual to offer it some extra energy boost. We can certainly do spellcraft without rituals, but it's often more potent to work with ritual so you can access energy that the mundane mind is often closed to and harness the powers of the external as well as the internal.

Elements of Ritual

Below I will describe the most popular elements of ritual in Hedge Witchcraft. Not all hedge witches use these elements, and some may have an entirely different system altogether. What I present here is what is well known to the Witchcraft community at large, along with the specific elements of Hedge Witchcraft.

Intention

First we need to decide what the intention is for the ritual. Let's say we want to honour the season of Beltane. So, we would like to perform a ritual that marks the start of the season on May Eve. We look at the symbology of the season, the gods and goddesses that we work with, and what is happening in nature, and we decide how to proceed in attuning ourselves to these forces through ritual. We must go into the ritual with the very clear intention of honouring Beltane, the start of summer here in the UK, the union of the God and Goddess, or however you see Beltane in your own tradition. Whatever the purpose of your ritual, make sure that the intention is clear.

Casting the Circle

After you have clarified your intention, you can cast a circle with that intention in mind. A circle is cast in order to create a space that is between the worlds—a signified place where the liminal exists. If you cast a circle in a liminal space, you have just added extra juice to your working.

Some use a circle to hold in the energies of their working, such as when spellcrafting, and then release it at a given point during the ritual. Others simply cast a circle to create a sacred space, a place where one can commune with the gods, strengthen their relationship with the elements, talk to the ancestors, etc. Ceremonial magicians cast circles in order to protect themselves from whatever it is that they are summoning, but that is not part of this simple folk practice. I have no desire or need to summon demons or other such creatures into my life and work; there are plenty of negative-type folk already in the world. Circle casting may or may not be necessary in your tradition, but let's have a look at it and see how it can work for you. You may choose to cast a circle for certain rituals and not for others.

Before you cast a circle, you may want to ritually cleanse the area. Some people see no need for this, as they are performing their ritual out in the wilds and feel that the energy of nature is pure and free from negativity already. Others feel that some areas may have a psychic residue, or lingering energy, perhaps from other workers of the arts who may have used the space, such as within well-known stone circles like the Rollright Stones in England. Many, many different workers of the art go there all the time, and you may want to clear the space for your own work. It is your choice.

If you are working from your home, you may or may not feel the need to cleanse the space. If you have a dedicated room or part of the garden that you use solely for this type of work, you may cleanse it once a month or once a year or once in a lifetime. Again, the choice is yours, and you will have to use your intuition to see what feels right. I have a room indoors that I sometimes use that is dedicated to my work and as such doesn't really need circle casting or cleansing.

You can use a broom, incense, water, song, chant, drumming, visualisation, and more to cleanse the area. You can also cleanse the area after the circle has been cast, which some people prefer.

To cast a circle, stand facing north and gather the energies of the land below you and the sky above you. Draw these energies in through your feet and the top of your head. When these energies are swirling within you, visualise the energy pouring out of you through your hand and your wand, stick, or stang; pointing at the ground, see it form a circle of light. I see this light as a bluish-white light. You can also extend this line into a globe so that you are enclosed within a bubble. This is not necessary, but some people prefer it.

You can cast the circle deosil (clockwise) or widdershins (counterclockwise). Some witches never cast widdershins, but I've always found this a bit strange; as the earth spins counterclockwise, which gives us our perception of the sun travelling clockwise across the sky, it seems odd to never want to move with the earth. You will have to see what feels right for you. Know, however, that if you ever work with others, clockwise will be the way most circles are cast.

*Some witches say that casting widdershins
is for banishing or baneful magic, while
deosil is for positive and nurturing
rituals. You may or may not agree.*

Next, the elements are called to join you in the circle. The elements are always there, of course, but you are really opening up your own awareness of them in your rite. Stand facing north, raise your arms, and say:

**I look to the north and call upon the element
of earth to be with me in my rite.**

Wait and feel the presence of the element of earth. Then turn to the east and say:

**I look to the east and call upon the element
of air to be with me in my rite.**

Do the same for the south/fire and the west/water.

Next, you can call upon the Fair Folk, the ancestors, and the Lord and Lady to be with you in your space and hallow and bless it. You can say:

> I call upon the Fair Folk, those who are in tune
> with my intention, to be with me in rite. May
> there always be friendship between us.
>
> I call upon the ancestors, those of blood, place,
> and tradition, to be with me in my rite.
>
> I call upon the Lady, the Mistress of Magic,
> Great Enchantress, and Earth Mother.
>
> I call upon the Lord, the Master of the
> Greenwood, Great Hunter, and Sky Father.

Don't just say the words; *feel* them. Otherwise, you might as well not speak any words at all. In fact, you don't even need to use words as you can say them in your mind or even just feel them. Stating things aloud does have its own power, however, in that they are manifesting through sound and vibration. I sometimes use words and sometimes do not. It depends on the mood of the ritual and the intention.

Everything that we have called out and connected to is now with us as part of us and our space. These are energies that you can call upon to aid you in your work or to simply attune with in a special way.

In order to take down the circle, you simply do everything in reverse and thank the Lord and Lady, the ancestors, the Fair Folk, and the elements. You can say something like:

> I give my thanks to the Lord and Lady for being
> with me in my rite. Goddess within and Goddess
> without, God within and God without, I honour
> you for all that you are with all that I am.

Ancestors, you whose blood runs through my veins, whose
stories flow through this land, whose laughter is heard
on the breeze, thank you for being with me in my rite.

To the Fair Folk, to those who guide and inspire me, I
thank you from the bottom of my heart for being with me
in my rite. May there always be friendship between us.

Turn to each direction in turn and say:

I look to the north and thank the element
of earth for being with me in my rite.

Repeat as appropriate for the other three directions and elements: east/
air, south/fire, and west/water. Alternately, use the appropriate elements
and directions that are suited to your particular locale.

To take down the circle, use the tool (or your hand) and simply gather
the energy back within you through the tool. Point it at the ground and
turn, either in the same direction you used while casting or the opposite
direction—whichever feels most comfortable. Gather the energy within.
Once the energy is pulled back into your body, you can ground it by sending it back into the ground and sky or you can use it to empower certain
tools, should you so wish. If you have an outdoor altar, this is a great way to
store any extra energy you may still feel after grounding.

Finally, you can speak a few words in closing, such as:

My rite here is done. Blessings upon this
land and upon all who dwell within.

Hallowing the Compass

This is another method of casting the circle found in traditional Witchcraft. You may prefer this method to the previous one or it may inspire you
to create your own method that feels appropriate in your work. Hallowing
the compass uses very few tools; in fact, it only uses the stang itself. Start
by placing the stang in the northern part of the circle. If it has a sharpened
point and the ground is soft enough, you can stick it in the earth itself.

Sometimes the ground simply is too hard in an area to do so, in which case you can have the stang with you, holding it at all times.

Move to the centre of the circle, facing north. Ground and centre (you can do the roots and branches meditation found in chapter 12), then gather up the energies of the earth into your body. Move to the northern edge of the circle, pick up your stang, and visualise energy flowing out of your body through the stang, creating a line of energy. Walk around the circle three times, letting this line of energy create a triple circle around you. You can then state the purpose of the ritual that is to be held within, such as this:

> **I cast this circle to be a place that is not a place,**
> **in a time that is not a time, to be a gateway**
> **to walk between the worlds.**

You might ask the Fair Folk to lend their aid to your rite and ask for their blessings.

Replace the stang in the northern part of the circle's edge. You may prefer to have it in the centre of your circle, say if you are doing the rite of treading the mill (more on that below). You might place your stang on the circle's edge that corresponds to the time of year; for instance, in the north for Yule, northeast for Imbolc, east for Ostara, southeast for Beltane, south for Litha, southwest for Lammas, west for Mabon, northwest for Samhain. Whatever works for you and has the most meaning is correct.

Now stand in the centre of the circle, facing north, and visualise a line of energy flowing from the sky, down into the top of your head and through your body, down into the earth. Then visualise another line of energy running across the circle through your body from east to west. This line could run through your solar plexus, your heart space, or your pelvic area. Finally, visualise a line running through your body from north to south, intersecting at the area where the other two lines already meet. All three lines meet and connect in your body at one point. Feel and see within your mind's eye a globe of energy as a sphere of light around you; each of these lines is connecting to an edge of that sphere.

These are the lines that connect you to the four corners of the globe. You are creating a microcosm of the macrocosm running through your body. It's a wonderful experience!

Next, call in the four directions. In a traditional practice, this would relate more to your local environment than to the classical associations. So, for me that would mean water to the east, fire to the south, earth to the west, and air to the north.

To take down the compass that you have created, simply do everything in reverse. Take the globe of energy back into your body. Release the lines of energy that run through your body. You might see them fading away into nothing or being pulled back into the directions from which they originated. Then walk around and gather up the perimeter of your circle through your stang. You might say something like "Gather in, gather in, all that has been here within" three times as you walk the circle three times, visualising the energy being pulled back into the stang. Ground and centre the energy that you used to create the circle back into the earth when you have finished.

Ritual Actions

When performing a ritual, you have a "sandwich" in which there is a middle part taking place between a beginning/setup and ending/take-down. This is the ritual action, the part where you bring the symbolism of the ritual to life. It can be a sabbat celebration, a hedge-riding experience, or a full moon esbat. This middle can be anything you want it to be.

This, essentially, is all there is to the hedge witch's ritual. It is simple and easy to perform, using minimal tools and relying on the individual's own talent to create a meaningful and honest rite. Later we will take a deeper look at what makes Hedge Witchcraft different from other Witchcraft traditions: that is, how to perform the art of hedge riding. First, though, let's look at the tools used by the hedge witch.

*T*he cycle has turned once again; another full year has passed. The hedge witch feels the cycles within cycles, the cycle of her soul dancing in the greater cycle of the seasons that dances in the cycle of the year and the cycle of the stars and planets. Each turning point where she can honour one moment flowing into another, one energy shifting and changing into a new energy, is a time for honouring and a time for ritual. She gathers her tools and heads out into the forest, the frost crunching under her feet and the darkness of winter looming overhead. Once at her special place, she will make an offering of poetry and song, as well as mead, to celebrate the turning of the year, blending her energy with that of the season and attuning herself through ritual to the magic that lies everywhere.

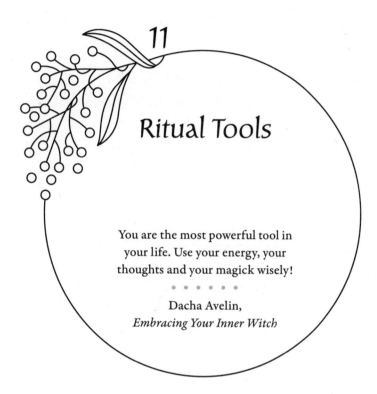

11

Ritual Tools

You are the most powerful tool in
your life. Use your energy, your
thoughts and your magick wisely!

• • • • • • •

Dacha Avelin,
Embracing Your Inner Witch

The tools used in Hedge Witchcraft are simple. You will not find elaborate swords and athames (ritual knives found most often in the Wiccan traditions), large swinging censers and ritual scourges. Instead, the tools of the hedge witch are those that she already has to hand and that she uses in her everyday life. These tools are used in both celebratory rituals as well as those involving hedge riding.

The tools for the hedge witch are:

- The stang/stick/wand (discussed in chapter 9)

- A sharp knife (for practical purposes, such as cutting or trimming branches, inscribing candles, etc.)

- Candles (outdoors I use candles in lanterns so they won't go out in the slightest breeze)

- A cup/goblet (to pour the shared offering into)

This, really, is all you need to practice the Craft.

I would even say that you truly don't need anything at all, but these items do come in handy for practical uses or as focal points.

The stang/stick/wand is used to cast the circle, substitutes as an altar in ritual when placed into the ground, and is used as a focal point in the rite of treading the mill (more on that in chapter 12). The knife is a practical item and really isn't used for magic, unlike the athame of Wicca. The candle, a symbol of the God, provides some light in the darkness of nighttime rituals. The cup/goblet, a symbol of the Goddess, is used to contain the libation or offering that is shared between you and the spirits of place, the ancestors, the Fair Folk, or the Lord and Lady.

Other tools include a broom, to sweep an area clear of leaves or debris (small handheld brooms are good for this, or even a bough of cedar or spruce) and to psychically cleanse an area. You can also sprinkle water to cleanse an area, so a small cup is necessary. You might sprinkle cleansing herbs as well, such as rosemary. I would advise against the old practice of sprinkling salt to cleanse a space when outdoors. Some witches cast their circles with salt, forming the outline of their circle with it. Only do this indoors if you feel it is necessary, as this is very damaging to the environment if done outdoors (though your floorboards also may not appreciate it very much). If you must use anything at all indoors, flour is better—or dried flowers and herbs or even a cord of some sort if you absolutely feel you must have a visual outline of your circle. When outdoors only use what you can take back with you.

Cauldrons can be used to contain small fires, though they can be a pain to lug around the countryside and are better used for back garden workings. Similarly, fire pits are a great tool for outdoor rites.

Some hedge witches like to use incense. I, for one, adore the smell of incense, but I cannot use it indoors because of my asthma. Some people may live in buildings that do not allow smoke of any kind. Instead of incense, I use scented beeswax or soy candles as this doesn't set off my asthma. Incense can create a wonderful mood to your rituals, and the scent can trigger your mind into the proper state to travel between the worlds. Incense also can be used to cleanse and purify an area. Loose incense is preferred, which is burned on a special incense-burning charcoal block (available from any metaphysical shop). A heatproof dish or container is necessary to hold the charcoal and burning incense. You can also use joss sticks, which are handy as they can be stuck straight into the ground, but do be careful in very dry areas. If you live with others who object to incense or smoke of any kind and you do not wish to burn candles, you can also make a water-based spray to cleanse an area. Fill a spray bottle with water and add four or five drops of lavender essential oil. Shake before you spray, and you can cleanse and scent your workspace easily and effectively.

Witches of any tradition love to have representations of special places or moments with them in the form of fetishes, which can be objects found on walks such as stones, feathers, flower petals, and the like. They may also carry or wear special charms (more on charms in chapter 12) or have special jewellery or clothing for their rites. Then again, they may simply wear the clothing that they have worn all day, for in times past, the chances of a simple witch having a special set of ritual clothes was pretty much nonexistent. Do whatever you feel like doing, whether that is having a beautiful robe or cloak or wearing jeans and your favourite T-shirt.

Some hedge witches have altars where they perform their spellcrafting and rituals. This may be indoors but is preferably outdoors. As stated earlier, the stang can represent an altar by simply sticking it into the ground, usually either in the north of the circle or in the centre. The lantern can also be hung from the stang's branches. The stang is wonderful because you have your own portable altar wherever you go. If indoors, you can place the stang in a bucket of sand or earth to keep it upright.

You can indeed make other portable altars, such as spreading a small cloth on the ground and having your favourite ritual items or spellworking ingredients upon it. These can be folded up, and some even have handy pockets sewn in that are used to carry tools and other ritual items. There are some patterns online for these handy little cloth altars, and they are available in metaphysical shops as well.

Other altars can be a stone in the forest or an old tree stump. You can set up a small altar in your back garden with some bricks and two-by-fours or visit a garden centre, where there are lots of stone benches and suchlike that can be used as altars. I found a lovely stone base that previously had a statue on it from an antique centre. The statue was long gone, but the base was there and is now one of my outdoor places of work and ritual. It has four dwarven faces looking out at each direction, which reminds me of the Norse myth of the four dwarves that hold up the corners the sky (Nordri, Austri, Sudri, and Vestri).

Indoors your altar could be a reinforced cardboard box with a nice cloth upon it or again some pieces of wood on top of some bricks. It could be an old chest or small coffee table. These are easily available at auction houses for next to nothing prices, often in beautiful old wood such as oak. Indoors I have a pine blanket box that doubles as my altar.

Other tools will be related to herbcraft or spellcrafting. You might like to have a mortar and pestle for grinding your herbs or a good collection of fabric and threads for spellcraft (see chapter 15). You will perhaps find that a small collection of items such as these begins to build up, so having a little cupboard or box to keep them all together in one place is very handy. You might have a small chest or a wall cupboard. Old smoking cabinets are fairly easy to come by and have little drawers and shelves and even places to hang small objects from where the pipes used to sit. Here in the UK you can buy large old Victorian cupboards and hanging wall cupboards for sometimes less than £20 at auction. "Brown furniture" is currently out of fashion, and my house is filled with gorgeous old Victorian and vintage furniture at bargain prices. Scour auctions (for great deals on furniture) and secondhand shops, as well as antique fairs and markets, and you will find the most wonderful things. I know I have. Most of everything that I have was not purchased brand new, and I prefer it that way: these items are being put to use again and have their own stories to tell.

The most important tool for the hedge witch is the mind. Combined with the will, you are able to travel between the worlds to work your magic and enchant your life however you see fit.

She leans into her stang and pushes the pointed end into the loamy soil of the forest floor. This will be her altar in the little forest clearing where she dances under the light of the moon and calls to her fairy allies. She steps back and the stang stays upright; then she takes the small garland of flowers that she made in her back garden out of her bag and gently places it on the top of the stang. She lights a candle in the lantern and places it at the foot of the stang, and her altar setup is complete. She breathes in the night air, the forest sounds around her hushed as if in anticipation. Suddenly an owl calls out from the trees overhead, signalling the time to begin. She moves slowly at first, dancing around the stang in a clockwise motion, calling the powers of nature to her in her rite. Overhead the moon looks on, blessing everything in its silvery light.

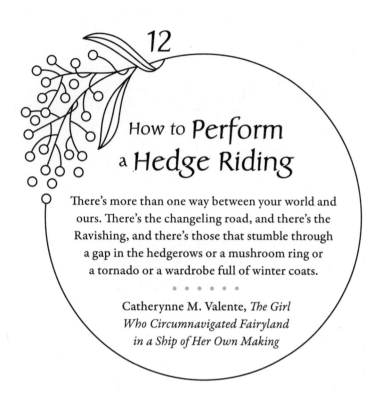

12

How to Perform a Hedge Riding

There's more than one way between your world and
ours. There's the changeling road, and there's the
Ravishing, and there's those that stumble through
a gap in the hedgerows or a mushroom ring or
a tornado or a wardrobe full of winter coats.

. . . . . .

Catherynne M. Valente, *The Girl
Who Circumnavigated Fairyland
in a Ship of Her Own Making*

Hedge riding can be performed within a ritual context. You have already
seen the elements of ritual, as well as the tools involved. When first starting
out in hedge riding, I highly recommend using ritual and casting a circle,
not in the least to get you familiar with the work but also to give you a
solid foundation for the hedge riding itself. Once you have been hedge riding for a couple of years, you may find that you need the ritual less and less
or you may find that your rituals change and develop with your Craft. Here
I will go through the process of hedge riding itself and offer some different
ways of entering into the trance state required to travel between the worlds.

When performing a hedge riding in ritual, you will have cast the circle
and created a space that is already between the worlds. Please note that it
is not always necessary to cast a circle in order to perform hedge riding

(as mentioned above); however, for those just starting out, this may be the preferred method, with the help of all that has been called into the circle to aid you in your work. A hedge riding can be performed indoors or out, depending upon your circumstances. Your own personal safety should always come first. If you live in a city and don't feel like you have a place outdoors to work, then you can do so from your own home. Houseplants can surround your ritual or working area, lending their energies to your work as well as being pretty and useful, with some houseplants—such as English ivy, the peace lily, or spider plants—helping clean the air.

Some people ask if there are any dangers to hedge riding. As with all things in Witchcraft, the answer is both yes and no. Snapping out of a trance too quickly can have physical and mental repercussions (more on this below). You may find yourself in situations in the otherworld that challenge you. What I will emphatically state is that what you bring along with you in your hedge-riding experience, you will find in the otherworld. For the otherworld lies over our own world, and they mirror each other in many ways. If you bring negative energies such as anger or hate, you will probably find that reflected in the otherworld. However, if you go with a positive intent and an open heart, you will learn many wonderful things and have magical experiences that help you to become a better witch and a better person.

You can protect yourself, should you feel the need, by casting a ritual circle. Your stang is also there not only to help you cross over to the otherworld but to protect you. You can take your stang (or your wand) with you on the astral as well as the physical.

To begin hedge riding, you will need to calm and centre your energy, otherwise known as grounding and centring. I like to do what I call the roots and branches meditation. Let's look at this starting point more closely.

Roots and Branches Meditation

Here I become aware of my heart energy and expand that energy down through my spine and into the earth. With every exhale I feel the energy expand like the roots of a tree deep into the earth beneath me. Then, breathing in, I take in the energy of the earth through my roots and pull it up through my body and out through the top of my head. This released energy forms branches that reach out as far above me as my roots do below me. With my next inhale, I breathe in the energies of the sky through my leaves and branches, and with my exhale the energy goes down into my body and out through my roots. This is then followed with an inhale through my roots and up my body and an exhale through the branches at the top. This is repeated for as long as I feel necessary in order to energise me and ground and centre my body. When I feel ready, I draw my roots and branches back into my body and my heart space, and with my hand in front of my body, I draw a vertical line from my head to my navel, cementing the centring process within my soul. I am now ready to work.

• • •

When performing a hedge riding, there are two different ways to go about it: in the astral and in the physical. I will begin with a discussion about the preparation for hedge riding in the astral before we get to the ritual itself. Hedge riding in the astral is where we send our consciousness into the otherworld while our bodies remain in this world. Later in this chapter we will also look at performing a hedge riding in the physical, as well as a full ritual to perform this variation. You can use a tool, such as your stang, to help you as you journey in both situations.

Hedge Riding in the Astral

When performing a hedge riding in the astral, you are sending out a large part of your consciousness into the otherworld while your physical body remains in this world. You will split your consciousness somewhat from your body in order to achieve this state, though you will not fully separate the two. As with similar trance states like hypnosis, one has the ability to come out of it at any time they desire, and they are not reliant on another to "bring them out." You will still have control over your physical body, and you will be able to react to things such as environmental stressors or threats. If the fire alarm is going off, if the dog starts barking madly, or if the baby starts crying, then you will be able to come out of the trance to react accordingly.

There is, however, a detriment to coming out quickly from any trance state. I came out of a hedge-riding experience on the astral too quickly one time and paid the price for it physically afterwards. I snapped back into my body and thought that it was fine; I didn't feel funny and got on with things. Nothing immediately happened. Twenty minutes later, however, I started to feel ill and wondered if I had eaten anything that had gone off at breakfast. Then I started vomiting and couldn't stop. It was just bile, but my body was reacting to the sudden shock of what I had been doing in my hedge riding. After about fifteen minutes of riding the porcelain bus, I lay on the bed and felt very sorry for myself. I then realised what I had done: I hadn't come back to my body in a way that wouldn't shock it. Normally I follow the process I had undertaken to go into the trance state except in reverse to come out that state. It's a gradual process that allows the body to adapt to the new feeling and sensation of having a large portion of the consciousness separated and far away. A sudden return has a physical effect, like standing up too quickly can make someone light-headed. Returning too quickly from a trance state affects not only your body, but your spiritual self too: both feel it and can respond badly. Needless to say, since then I have taken care when coming out of a trance, as I never want to repeat that situation. I urge you to learn from my experience so that you don't ever have to go through that either!

So, after calming and centring the physical and spiritual self, you are now ready to embark upon a hedge-riding experience. Ensure that you won't be distracted or interrupted, and also ensure that you are comfortable enough for the undertaking. You may be hedge riding for twenty minutes to an hour, so being warm/cool enough, sitting in a comfortable seat so that you don't restrict any blood flow, and having a quiet space are essential when first starting out. I like to sit cross-legged on the floor, but I use several cushions to raise my bottom off the ground so that my legs and feet don't start to go numb halfway through the experience. As well, it's also easier on the hip and knee joints. I have also used a high kneeling-posture meditation cushion. If you need to move halfway through your journey for comfort, you can do so, but make it as quick as possible while maintaining that link to the otherworld. If you are using a chair, have your feet flat on the floor and try to sit upright without using the back of the chair. This will keep you more awake. If, however, you do doze off during a hedge riding, don't worry. This experience can be just as informative as one when you are awake. When you wake up, come back to yourself slowly, then try to recall any dreams you had. Write them down immediately. And next time ensure that you're well rested.

The Norse tradition of seidr involved the seeress sitting upon a chair that was usually raised on a platform. Small charms of cushioned chairs have been found in archaeological digs, and these are thought to have been symbols of seidr and the craft of the seeress, the völva. In the Celtic artwork of the Gundestrup cauldron, we see the figure of a man, presumed to be Cernunnos, sitting cross-legged while communing with all manner of creatures around him, both mythical and mundane. Buddha achieved enlightenment through sitting under the Bodhi tree. It seems that seated postures to achieve various spiritual endeavours are known all over the world, and hedge riding is no exception.

Grounding after Hedge Riding

After each hedge-riding session, it's a good idea to ground yourself fully so that you are totally back in this world. Eating something is probably the best thing you can do, but if you don't have any food with you, you can stamp your feet on the ground or clap your hands and say your name three times out loud. This will remind your body and your soul that you have returned, and you won't feel "spaced out" afterwards.

Giving an Offering

After each hedge-riding experience—or before if that works better for you—it is good manners to give an offering of some kind. The giving of an offering demonstrates that you are willing to offer something in return for the knowledge and experience you have gained in your work. Offerings such as bread, honey, milk, or even just water can be made with the heartfelt intention of deepening that relationship and the dedication to working and walking between the worlds. You can also offer a poem or a song or something that you have personally made with your own hands. If you are leaving a physical offering, ensure that it won't adversely affect the wildlife or the environment. For example, never leave chocolate as an offering, as it can be harmful to wildlife.

Entering a Trance State

Hedge riding is all about working with different trance states. Some people might find that they have difficulty at first in achieving a trance state or separating their consciousness sufficiently to work and walk between the worlds. Here are some ideas to help you become more comfortable in this area.

ROCKING BACK AND FORTH. Either seated or standing, rocking back and forth or even swaying for a minute or two can help you to relax your "talking mind" and loosen up your body so that you are able to move into the proper state for hedge riding.

CHANTING OR SINGING A SPECIAL SONG TO SHIFT YOUR CONSCIOUSNESS. You can create a special song or chant. If you come across a song or lyric that you feel works to help you shift into a different space, then use it.

DRUMMING. Playing a specific drumbeat or listening to a recorded one can help you shift into that trance state.

DANCING. Moving your body frees your mind. Dancing for a few minutes can help you relax and open up your awareness.

HAND GESTURES USED ONLY WHEN HEDGE RIDING. You can develop your own hand gestures to take you to that special state of mind needed when hedge riding. You might adapt some Eastern hand mudras or invent your own that have special meaning to you.

HERBAL AIDS. I do not advocate the use of drugs of any sort when hedge riding. However, if you would like to use certain herbs to help you relax (and stay hydrated), I recommend drinking mugwort or vervain tea before you perform a hedge riding. Talk to your doctor or herbalist before taking any herbs if you are pregnant or on medication.

TREADING THE MILL. This is a wonderful tool to enter a trance state. It is an excellent alternative way to perform a hedge-riding experience, so let's look at it in further detail below.

Treading the Mill

In traditional Witchcraft you'll often see the term *treading the mill*. This involves a witch's movement around a stationary object, usually the stang, but it can be anything: a fire, a stone, or a tree, for example. In Hedge Witchcraft, using a staff or stang is ideal, for it stands as a representation of the world tree, a symbol of the hedge you will ride to take you to the otherworld.

It works best if the bottom of the stang is sharpened slightly so that you can push it into the soil and it can stand upright by itself. Where I live, in the summer the soil can sometimes become very hard, and so occasionally I have to use a small hand trowel to create a crack in the earth that I can then push the stang into and have it stand upright. If you have to work indoors, then you can use a large bucket of sand and push the stang into that to have it remain in the upright position, or even perhaps use a Christmas tree stand.

It is customary to have a lantern at the base of the stang, but you can also hang it from one of the tines. You can also hang a garland of flowers and foliage from the tines corresponding to the season at hand.

Once everything is in place, you can cast a circle or hallow the compass; then you are ready to tread the mill. In the north, face forwards as if you were about the walk around the circle normally (clockwise or counterclockwise; your choice). Then turn your head slightly inwards so that you can keep your gaze on the stang in the centre. Begin to move forwards, keeping your head and eyes on the central focal point. If this is too uncomfortable for you, then you can adapt the traditional pose to the following: stand facing the centre of the circle and begin to move sideways. One of the best ways to do this is through a grapevine step: step across the front with your right foot, sideways with the left, behind with the right, sideways with the left. This will propel you sideways in a clockwise motion. Reverse the steps if you want to move counterclockwise.

Begin to pick up the pace while keeping your focus on the stang at the centre of your circle. Allow your thoughts to remain on the stang, sensing the power of the world tree flowing through it. Faster and faster you move, your gaze ever fixed upon the stang. You may see it begin to glow with its own light or seem to fade from sight altogether. Go with it. Feel the veil between the worlds thinning. When you feel the time is right and you have worked up enough energy to cross between the worlds, stop. You may drop to the ground, you may fall to your knees, you may sit cross-legged on the ground. Close your eyes. You might see a tree before you with a door in its trunk or you may feel your body taking a running leap over a low hedge or the stang itself turning into a portal. Step through the veil and into the otherworld. When you are ready to return, come back to your body slowly, not rushing the process. Stand up, move to the stang, and touch it in reverence. Then bend down, touch the earth, and ground any extraneous energy into the earth. Leave an offering, open the circle, and your work is done.

Hedge riding is a ritual action that can accompany any ritual at any time. The more time you spend working in the otherworld, the easier it will be to access. Do be careful, however, with the amount of hedge riding that you do, for too much can leave you feeling "spaced out," or not fully in this world. While it's perfectly normal to feel that you can cross and walk between the worlds at any time, to not be fully present in this world can have its own repercussions. You need to be fully in this world while driving, for example, both for your own sake and that of everyone else on the road. Also it is important to come fully back to this world and not dwell in a state of limbo. While we honour the liminality of Hedge Witchcraft, we are also very practical and know that we must live in this world even as we are able to visit the otherworld through our Craft.

Go over the words of the ritual that you would like to perform until you can remember the sequence of events. Alternatively, you may record yourself reading the text, allowing for pauses, then play it back during the ritual. However, working from memory is much better and will flow easier. As well, electronic devices often have a tendency to malfunction when magic is afoot. Or you may take the following as a suggestion and create your own ritual that is relevant to you and your location, using local folklore and the natural landscape.

Hedge-Riding Ritual to Enter the Otherworld

This ritual can be used as a guide for your first hedge-riding experience. I will write the sequence out in full, and you can then use this format for further workings. This hedge riding will be performed in the astral, so you should find a good, quiet space in which to work. You can perform this ritual indoors or out, as long as you are in a safe space and will not be interrupted. If, for any reason, you are interrupted, don't worry; the heavens won't come crashing down. Simply take some deep breaths, ground and centre again, and depending on how you feel, either start the ritual again, join back in where you left off if you can and it feels right, or save it for another time. This hedge-riding experience is done seated either on a chair or on the ground, in whatever position you find the most comfortable.

Feel free to adapt this ritual to incorporate other methods of entering the trance state required for hedge riding mentioned previously:

- Ground and centre using the roots and branches meditation
- Cast your circle or hallow the compass using your preferred method
- Settle yourself and prepare to walk between the worlds

Take up your stang or staff and hold it before you. If you are seated, have the stang or staff between your legs. Hold it with both hands firmly but not overly so. Take a deep breath, then strike the ground three times with the bottom of the stang or staff. This is the signal for the working to begin. Then, keeping the stang or staff upright before you, with its tip on the ground, pull it gently towards you until you feel it is in a comfortable position. You may lean the top of the stang or staff towards your head a little, which may activate the area often known as the third eye. You might feel a tingling in this area, which is a good sign that you are ready to work. You might feel the stang or staff humming with energy, becoming rooted in the ground while reaching for the heavens above. You might feel the body of the stang or staff merging with your own, giving you a sense of what the world tree feels like. Each person's experience will be unique. Go with it.

When you are ready, it is now time to ride the hedge. Close your eyes and see a mist forming in front of you. Walk into the mist, which slowly begins to clear. Before you there is a tunnel of green, a wonderful place where two hedges meet, arching overhead. The inside of the green tunnel is dark, but you can see a glowing light at the end. You might like to say a prayer before you enter the enclosed space within the hedge—perhaps a few words to the deities or even a little incantation, such as:

> *Between the worlds am I*
> *Between the land and sky*
> *I walk with footsteps true*
> *To bring myself to you*
> *Through this hedge I go*
> *To learn what I need to know*

Hold your desire to enter the otherworld firmly in your soul, then walk through the hedge. Follow the green hollow towards the light of the otherworld. Once you have stepped through and into the light, take note of what you see and take time to adjust to your new surroundings. What time of day is it? How does the land flow? Can you see any landmarks, animals, or people? Observe silently for a while. Understand how your body feels in the otherworld. Does it feel lighter? Heavier? Look down at your hands. Do they appear as normal or is your skin shining with an inner light? Are they transparent? There is no right or wrong in the otherworld, only your own personal experience that is individual to you.

Find a destination point that you can see from where you are standing and make your way towards it. A forest, a hill, a lake: all these may appear before you. Spend some time at that place just being in the landscape, becoming a part of the landscape. As a walker between the worlds, this place might feel like home to you. It might be utterly familiar or it might be totally different from what you expected. Explore for a few minutes, knowing that you are guided by the ancestors, the deities, the elements, and those of the otherworld itself. If you come across someone, be polite. Do not spend too long in the otherworld as this is your first attempt on the astral, and after ten or fifteen minutes make your farewells and come back to this world.

You can see the hedge from which you entered the otherworld, and you make your way towards it. You see the tunnel, and you enter, walking back from where you came, the light guiding you back towards this world. You may say another prayer or incantation to come back to this world, such as:

Back to my own world I go
Back to the lands I do know
I walk with footsteps sure and true
To bring myself back to you
Through this hedge I return
And remember what I have learned

You step out into the mist, which slowly clears to reveal that you are back in this world. Take a deep breath and slowly open your eyes. Wiggle fingers on the stang or staff. Wiggle your toes, moving your legs slightly. Arch your back, taking another deep breath. Slowly lift up the stang or staff a couple of inches off the ground, and then, with intention, strike it three times upon the ground. This is the signal for the working to end. Gently put down your stang or staff and stretch out fully in your body. Eat or drink something if you feel it necessary, leave an offering, and then write down your experience in your journal as soon as you can in order to not forget a single detail. Even the smallest detail might be significant in future hedge ridings. Take down your circle if you have cast one, then relax for a while, letting the experience settle in your soul.

After your first hedge-riding experience, you may find that your dreams become more vivid or that things begin to happen with a newfound synchronism in your life. This is perfectly normal, for you are awakening your soul to your innate capacity to walk and work between the worlds. Your soul has been awakened to its true calling, and it is time to stand in your power and work your Craft.

Hedge Riding in the Physical

You can also perform hedge riding in the physical. In this state, your consciousness is not separated from your body, but rather you are taking it all with you as you cross over into the otherworld. Your spirit and your body are all going together through to the otherworld. In order to do so, you will physically need to be outside in the natural world. We'll go over this in detail here.

Find a place, preferably out in the wild and away from other folk. Search out through ordinance survey maps and online where some power spots in the landscape might be, such as ancient burial sites, ley lines, and such, or simply find a place that speaks to your soul. Liminal places—those in-between places that are neither one nor the other—are ideal. You might find locations such as at the beach, where the water meets the earth and sky, or on a hilltop. You might find the edge of a forest that opens onto a meadow or an open glade in woodland. And, just in case you forgot, you can also use a hedge! Liminal times are also great times to perform a hedge riding, both in the physical and the astral. Just before dawn, at dusk, or at midnight when it's neither one day nor the next are great times. If you are by the sea, you can also use the turning of the tides, when one tide turns into the next, from ebb to flow and vice versa.

I like to go out onto the heathland to do a hedge riding in the physical. There are a couple of routes I can take that have entrance points. One is through a tunnel of hedging where two hedges meet and through which a footpath runs straight down the middle. Another is an entrance about 50 feet from the road where there is a path onto the heath that starts by diving deep through some gorse bushes. I have also done hedge riding at an ancient tumuli as well as in my own back garden.

To begin, ground and centre yourself as you would when performing a hedge riding in the astral. Use the roots and branches meditation. This can be done before you leave the house. Take up your stang, staff, or wand, if you wish, to help you on your journey. Then, when you get to where you feel is a good liminal place to begin—such as at a hedgerow, a gate on a path, a hawthorn tree (beloved of the Fair Folk), or a gap between two trees—do the following exercise.

Repeat your intention for the hedge-riding experience, either out loud or in your mind. Then turn widdershins (counterclockwise) on the spot while feeling yourself leaving this world and connecting to the otherworld. In your mind's eye, see the mist at the gateway to where you want to walk coming through on the physical plane. Note where you are with new eyes, and when you take your first steps into the mist and beyond, know that you are now passing through a gateway and into the otherworld.

The otherworld lies over our own world, and you may come across creatures from both on your journeys. You may come across dog walkers from our own world as well as the Fair Folk and fellow creatures. Remember that your consciousness is working in two worlds, even as your body is walking in two worlds. This is the power and the advantage of being a hedge witch.

*Really take note of what you see, for anything
and everything might be significant. Go softly
and quietly. Walk lightly and in harmony with
the world around you. Don't worry about getting
into trouble, such as falling into a ditch or wading
into a pond, because your consciousness is still
working in this world and the otherworld. In fact,
you might even find that you have a heightened
sense of awareness to everything around you.*

You may notice that animals don't run away from you or may even approach you or just watch you from a certain vantage point. Just be still and allow it to happen. Looking into a deer's eyes is a wonderful experience. Do take the necessary precautions, however. Don't get too close to certain animals, such as stags during rutting season, or approach bears or coyotes in the wild. They may cross your path and you may feel blessed by that encounter, but equally don't push your luck.

You may notice glimpses of movement in the trees or in the shadows of hedgerows or behind stones. These may very well be the Fair Folk coming to assess you for the first time while you are in their territory. Have an open heart, and let it be known that you wish to establish a relationship with them. We will look at a ritual to connect with one of the Fair Folk as your guide and teacher in chapter 13.

When you are ready to leave the otherworld—and on the first attempt, a half hour to an hour is plenty—then return to where you began the journey. You might like to leave an offering in this world before you return to yours. As you approach the gateway that you used to enter the otherworld, see the mist once again forming. Stop, give thanks for what you have experienced, and then turn around on the spot three times, this time turning deosil (clockwise). Then walk through the gateway and know that you are back in your own world. Journal your experiences as soon as you are able.

Sometimes you may not be able to use the same entrance and exit points. If this is the case, find a marker beforehand that you can use to return to this world. It is good to scout out the area before working and find these locations so that you can enter and leave quickly if necessary. You can always snap back to this world simply by willing it to be so, but remember that sometimes there are physical and spiritual consequences for doing this sort of action (though not always; it depends on the situation). When I walk on the heath, I use different entry and exit points for my otherworldly journeys. I enter though the gorse bushes on one side of the heath and exit through a hollow where two hawthorns meet on the other side of the landscape. This allows me to travel further in the area without having to retrace my steps back to my original position. I still take my time and am careful that I am returning fully through this other portal from the otherworld. When you are just starting out, you may like to enter and return through the same gateway for the first few times before you really begin to get the hang of this working. Soon you will be hedge riding like it's second nature!

When performing a hedge riding on the physical plane, you are walking the landscape in this world and finding the places where you may pass through body and soul. Search out these places in your environment beforehand: it might be a hedge in your garden, a lone hawthorn tree in the wilds, a secluded beach (make note of the tides), a hilltop, a forest glade, an ancient burial mound, or whatever calls to you that speaks of the otherworld. Read up on your local folklore to discover the places where the veil is thin, and you will be able to move physically into the otherworld too.

• • •

As you can see, there are various ways to perform a hedge riding. No one way is better than the other. Find out what method works best for you in your practice and in your locality. Now let's look at some further rituals that you can do in your hedge riding.

*S*he drops to the ground and closes her eyes. As
she breathes heavily from her dance, she rides
her heartbeat across to the otherworld. The stang
grows and branches outwards, forming an arch she
can travel through. She leaves her physical body and
steps out and through the arch, calling to her fairy
companion to meet her. Once on the other side, she
is greeted with bright starlight and rolling hills. She
hears the tune her fairy companion plays upon his
flute and follows the sound down into the valley...

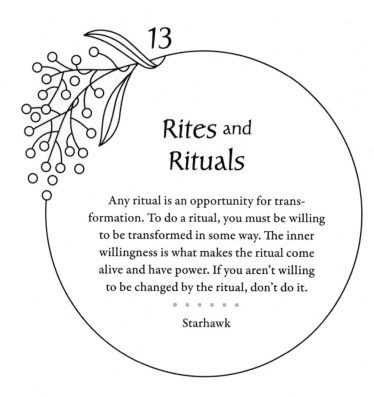

13

Rites and Rituals

Any ritual is an opportunity for transformation. To do a ritual, you must be willing to be transformed in some way. The inner willingness is what makes the ritual come alive and have power. If you aren't willing to be changed by the ritual, don't do it.

• • • • • • •

Starhawk

In this chapter I will provide you with further rituals that you can use in your own practice or from which you can develop your own or use as inspiration. These rituals are not ancient practice but come from years of research combined with my own experience and experimentation to see what works for me and what doesn't work in my own Craft. None of these rituals are set in stone, and they can all be adapted to better suit your needs and your work. Some involve hedge riding and others are celebratory rituals in which a hedge riding can take place if you so wish.

Finding Your Fylgja (Guardian)

Once you have entered the otherworld, you can then ask for your *fylgja* to be known to you. A fylgja (plural *fylgjur*) is a term from the Scandinavian traditions that denotes a being who acts as a guardian to an individual from

171

the time of their birth all the way through to their death. Fylgjur often appear in animal form, though they may take on other appearances. A fylgja is a spirit ally that can travel between the worlds with you. It is with you in this world and in the otherworld. Some people in other traditions might call them "power animals," but this is not quite the same. You do not denote your power from your fylgja, rather, your fylgja protects and guides you on the physical and astral planes. They are not "totem animals" either, for this has a different meaning that usually relates to a tribe, most widely known from the First Nations and Native American traditions. Sometimes the fylgja can be a bit of a shapeshifter and appear in human or fairy form.

This ritual is best performed on the astral, but you may want to take it to the physical for confirmation in a later ritual if you find that your fylgja is an animal that can be found in your location. Equally, you may simply find that after performing this ritual on the astral, your fylgja begins to appear to you on the physical plane more and more throughout your life, either physically or symbolically.

- Ground and centre using the roots and branches meditation
- Cast your circle or hallow the compass using your preferred method
- Settle yourself and prepare to walk between the worlds

Ride the hedge to the otherworld, using the ritual framework already provided in the previous chapter or adjusted to suit you and your own preferences. Once on the other side, go to a place that you have visited previously, a place that you were drawn to, and be there for a few moments, attuning yourself to the place. Then, when you are ready, state these words or something similar:

> *My fylgja/guardian I wish to be known*
> *I know that I do not walk alone*
> *For they have always been with me*
> *Now and back to my infancy*

Appear to me now and be true
So that I may come to know you

Wait; you will see your fylgja appear. It might be a bit shadowy or ethereal at first, but that's perfectly fine. As you get to know them more and more, they will grow in substance. It may take several attempts before you can see them clearly, so you may have to repeat this ritual a few times. Once they are clear to your perception, spend some time with them. It can simply be in silence, sitting together and being in each other's company. Remember, they have been with you since birth and have kept you company for many years. Now that you are aware of their form, take your time and get to know them. You might try to speak to them, but it may take a few attempts before you are able to hear them. As you have only just perceived them in your life, it may take some time before you can hear and understand them. Don't rush it.

When you have spent some time with your fylgja, thank them and return back to this world through the hedge. Go out into nature and place a suitable offering for your fylgja in a beautiful spot. Ensure that your next hedge-riding experiences are to deepen the connection to your fylgja and learn more about them. Eventually, you will be able to work with your fylgja to gain knowledge through them if you allow them to teach you what you need to know. You may be able to see through their eyes, to learn what it is that they know, and garner even more experience with the otherworld through working with them. Indeed, this may be the real form of shapeshifting that witches were said to be able to perform. Coming to know and working with your fylgja will bring you great benefits in your Craft.

When I first met my fylgja, I could see right through her; she appeared as a misty figure on the edge of my consciousness while I was in the otherworld. As I journeyed more and more to meet her in the otherworld, she appeared stronger in substance to my eyes. Even as I was doing this over several weeks, she also appeared to me on the physical plane, in this world, which shocked me to my core, for in the otherworld I saw her as a pure white doe, which is extremely rare. And not long after, a pure white doe appeared on the heath where I live, looking at me with knowing eyes that come straight from the otherworld.

Finding Your Fairy Companion

This is probably one of the most important rituals in your practice. Many witches work with otherworldly folk and have companions or what is sometimes known as fairy familiars. These are folk from the otherworld that are willing to work with you and offer guidance and sometimes protection. Know that this isn't a one-way street. You may be asked to help them as well, or perform certain actions such as specific offerings or the maintenance of a site, keeping it physically clean and the energies clear. You will be making a real and genuine bond with someone from the otherworld who will be your friend. Therefore, this relationship must be filled with mutual respect. To show the Fair Folk that you are willing and ready to work with them, it is wise to make an offering to them before undertaking this ritual.

Cast your circle using your preferred method. Ready yourself for a hedge-riding experience, perhaps using the roots and branches meditation. Take up your staff, strike the ground three times, and then, when you are ready, ride the hedge to the otherworld as you have done previously. Know and see your fylgja with you, as they always are. Once you have crossed the hedge, you find yourself in the otherworld.

Stand for a moment and settle within this landscape for a while. Then, softly but with confidence and assurance, ask that your companion from the Fair Folk be made known to you. You might hear music that you can follow or see a light in the distance. Your companion might appear before you, arriving in sparkling green motes of light. Note how they appear: they might look quite human or be very otherworldly. They might have different-coloured skin or hair than normal or their eyes or ears might appear different. They might glow with an inner light, like starlight. They might even appear in animal form, usually as an animal that is pure white or unusual in colour. Greet them with respect and ask if they are to be your guide and companion between the worlds. If the answer is affirmative, then allow the conversation and experience to flow. Note how your fylgja reacts to them. They will reassure you that you have found the right companion or warn you away from any potential danger.

Your fairy companion might tell you their name or you may have to try and guess it. They may only reveal their name after a few meetings, to see if you truly are ready to work with them. If the response is negative regarding them being your companion, then politely disengage, say farewell, and move on, trying again if you so wish. After you have spent some time (but not too much yet) in this attempt, return to this world in the same manner previously provided. Say your farewells, honouring those of the otherworld, and come back fully. Strike the ground three times with your stang or staff, then record the experience as soon as you can.

If you were unable to connect to your otherworld companion on the first attempt, do not worry. It may take several attempts before contact is made. They might be assessing your worth, ensuring that you are making a good effort, which will translate into a good relationship.

Remember that the otherworld does not owe you any favours. Sometimes we are like one on a quest and must show our worth before we are granted the information and relationships that we seek.

Once you have established contact with your companion, ensure that you maintain the relationship. Like any friendship, the best ones are those that have strong bonds. Meeting up with them at the solstice and then forgetting about them until the next festival isn't quite cutting it. You have got to make the effort to be present, honour them, and want to work with them, and you will see that returned in kind. No one likes to be called on for help and then ignored until help is needed once more. A good relationship is one of give and take, of reciprocity and kindness. Make regular offerings such as food or drink. Ask your companion what offerings are suitable; they will guide you. Ask them what places and times are best to meet with them, and they will work with you to the best of their abilities. They will tell you of the places in your landscape where there is hidden power. They will tell you where the herbs grow that you need in your work for your spells or reveal to you the chants and songs that take your soul on journeys you could not even imagine. They will guide your soul to its fullest potential.

Meeting with the Goddess and God

Hedge riding can be used to meet with the Goddess and the God. In this ritual, you will be taken to meet with the Lord and Lady of the Greenwood. This hedge riding is performed on the astral.

- Ground and centre using the roots and branches meditation
- Cast your circle or hallow the compass using your preferred method
- Settle yourself and prepare to walk between the worlds

Once through the hedge, you find yourself in the otherworld, your fylgja at your side. You may ask your fylgja to lead you to meet with the Lord and Lady of the Greenwood, or find your fairy companion to help you; either is perfectly acceptable. You may decide to seek out the Lord and Lady on your own. If so, you will have to have confidence in your being in the otherworld, and your intention must be perfectly clear. You might say something like:

> *I now desire to meet with the Lord and Lady of the Greenwood.*
> *May my footsteps lead me to them*
> *May my heart turn towards them*
> *May my eyes gaze upon them*
> *So may it be*

You will eventually find yourself in a large wood, the green light shining through the thick trunks of an ancient forest. Coming to a clearing, you hear the sounds of a little stream and birdsong trilling through the air. The earth feels solid under your feet. Your heart is awakened by a love of this place and all who dwell within it. You then say the following words, or something similar, to invoke the Lord and Lady into your life and make yourself known to them, who have always been there, waiting:

> *Hail to my Lady of the Green*
> *Who walks with twisted staff*
> *The Hosts of Faery following*
> *Bringing life unto the land*
> *The fullness and the blossom*
> *The lushness and the ripening*
> *I honour you with all that I am*
> *My Lady of the Green*
>
> *My Lord of the Forest*
> *Of all that is wild and free*
> *Of mirth and abandon*
> *And the Hosts of Faery*
> *Keeper of the Mystery*
> *Guardian of the Land*
> *I honour you, Lord of the Forest*
> *With all that I am*

There, next to a large rock in the warm sunlight, are two figures dressed all in green. You approach them and turn your face and heart towards them. What they tell you is what you need to know …

• • •

When you are ready, ride the hedge back to this world after thanking all those with whom you have journeyed. This hedge riding is so unique to the individual that I cannot possibly describe it for you in any more detail, for what the Lord and Lady say to you is for your ears alone. Know that you can return to them at any time and that they know you and love you. Show them that you are worthy of that love.

Full Moon Ritual

Here is a full moon ritual into which you may or may not incorporate a hedge-riding experience. It is totally up to you as to what you do with your esbat rituals! You may simply use them to honour the beauty and magic of the full moon, perform a hedge riding, or use the energy for spellcrafting and so on.

Here is a basic full moon ritual outline.

- Ground and centre using the roots and branches meditation
- Cast your circle or hallow the compass using your preferred method
- Call to the Goddess and the God
- Honour the time and season: which moon are you in, what is happening in nature in your location
- Draw down the moon (see below for details on this)
- Work any spells or perform a hedge riding
- Give an offering
- Close down the ritual space

Within some traditions of Witchcraft, we see forms of aspecting deity, which is to say that we bring or allow for deity to come into our bodies and our minds during ritual. This is most often seen in the rite of "drawing down the moon," which many coven-based traditions use at the time of the full moon. Here, the Goddess is invited to come into the high priestess and they then can provide oracular guidance and prophecy or simply give advice for each member. Some traditions also use "drawing down the sun" to aspect the male energies of the sun, which the hedge witch can certainly do as well. Sabbats are the best times for this rite.

Can drawing down the moon be performed solo in a Hedge Witchcraft tradition? Of course it can. You don't need anyone to invoke the deities within you, for you can do that all by yourself. While what the hedge witch does in drawing down the moon might alter slightly from a coven-based practice, it still is perfectly acceptable and valid for the solitary practitioner to feel the presence of the Goddess within themselves and work to strengthen their relationship with deity in this manner.

This is a beautiful and powerful rite within a ritual. You may find some written sources or people telling you that you should only perform this after years of working in the Craft or that you cannot perform this rite as a solitary. To this, I would say that as long as you are ready to meet with the Goddess and have already made yourself known to her, then there is nothing to fear, and you will gain a strengthening relationship with her by doing this rite regularly. Anyone can open their hearts and souls to deity in ritual, and this rite provides a good vehicle to feeling her deeply. Remember, she is always with you, just as the God is always with you, for in Witchcraft we believe that deity is immanent, both within and without.

To draw down the moon in ritual as a hedge witch, begin with casting your circle in the usual way. You may or may not feel the need to ride the hedge for this experience. Personally, I don't do a hedge riding to draw down the moon. I don't need to travel to the otherworld to draw down the moon; it happens right here in this world.

Stand beneath the moon and open yourself to its lunar energies. You can open your soul with a heartfelt prayer, raising your hands toward the moon and asking the Goddess to come into your being, and you may even state clearly the purpose for which you are inviting her, such as seeking prophesy or healing. You may feel the Goddess's energy filling your being with a cool, blue-white light. You might feel utterly calm, peaceful, and at one with the universe. You might feel a cool wave of love wash over you. You might envision parts of your life that have special meaning to you, and special people, and see the Goddess in all of these things. If you have asked for something specific, you will feel a certain energy touching that request. Know that your petition has been answered and that it is now up to you to instigate the change you need in your life, blessed by the touch of the Goddess herself. You have set your own sense of self aside so that she may enter your soul to give you what you need in that moment, and that is something truly special.

When you are ready, thank the Goddess and lower your hands, feeling the energy of the Goddess easing. Her powerful force fades into a nourishing stream of love, peace, and energy from which you can take action in your life and work your Craft for the betterment of all. It is especially useful just before performing spellcrafting, for you can send the energy of the Goddess into your working. Use her energy and blessing wisely.

Sabbat Rituals

Celebrating the sabbats are a good way to stay attuned to what is happening in the natural world. We can sometimes get distanced from the natural cycles, and both sabbats and esbats bring us back into the rhythm of the seasons. We remember that we are a part of the ever-flowing spiral of life, the great cycles of ebb and flow, of change and transformation.

Here is a basic sabbat ritual outline:

- Ground and centre using the roots and branches meditation
- Cast your circle or hallow the compass using your preferred method
- Call to the Goddess and the God
- Honour the time and season: Which sabbat are you celebrating and why? What is happening in nature in your location?
- Draw down the sun (similar to how you draw down the moon)
- Perform ritual act
- Work any spells or perform a hedge riding
- Give an offering
- Close down the ritual space

Sabbats usually contain a ritual act within them that symbolises what is happening at that particular point in the Wheel of the Year. They may stem from local folklore or you may begin a new tradition that is relevant to you and your location. It is best to create sabbat celebrations that are relevant to your local area. Therefore, I won't provide a complete set of sabbat rituals here, but I will offer some ideas for each one as well as ritual acts that you can try out in your own practice. You may or may not work a hedge riding for the sabbats, depending on whether you simply want to celebrate the turning of the cycle or use the energies for Craft workings. Either way is fine!

• • •

Some ideas for sabbat ritual acts include, but aren't limited to:

SAMHAIN: Welcome the Wild Hunt with a wild dance, poetry, or song. Run through the landscape at dusk. Symbolise the handing over of energies of the seasons from one deity to another, i.e., from the Oak King to the Holly King. You might have two wands, one of oak and one of holly, and for the next six months use the appropriate wand to invoke deity. Say a prayer for the ancestors and pay your respects to all those who have passed on this year. Light a candle with the intention that they all pass through unhindered into the otherworld. Try apple bobbing; once you have grasped the symbol of the otherworld within your teeth, take a big bite and savour your work with the otherworld.

YULE: Honour the longest night by spending time in darkness. At dawn light a candle to bring the sun's return back into your spiritual life as well as your physical life. Watch the sunrise and make it a part of your ritual act. Ask the Lord and Lady to bless a bough of evergreens, then bring it into your home to send its energy out until Twelfth Night, where you can then place it on the fire and send it back to deity.

IMBOLC: Have a bowl of milk (cow, sheep, oat, etc.) and ask for the Lady's blessing upon it. Then drink the milk and have it "in the belly," literally taking in her blessings. Make Brighid's crosses (see my work *The Book of Hedge Druidry* or look at some tutorials online) and bless them in ritual, then hang them throughout the home. Reconsecrate or bless your working tools and candles.

OSTARA: Draw or paint symbols of your magical intention onto a hardboiled egg and then bless it with the light of the sun and the powers of the east at dawn. Keep it on your altar for a while or eat it and literally take in the blessings! Craft hares made of felt beforehand (whole kits are now available in craft shops and online), and bless them in ritual. Decorate the home and your altar with them during spring to bring about good luck, abundance, and magical enchantment.

BELTANE: Make an offering for the Fair Folk and your fairy companion specifically. Braid three ribbons of different colours in a magic spell to bring what you desire into your life, perhaps chanting with each plait. Light a fire outdoors to signal the start of summer or to welcome its eventual coming. Light a torch from this fire and process around the outside of your property with it to bring in blessings and protection. If you can't have a fire and torch, light a candle and place it in a lantern, then process around your property/house.

LITHA: Make an offering to the Fair Folk in some wild and lonely place. Walk the land as part of your ritual, feeling the magic of the summer solstice within the earth and all around you. Watch the sunrise or sunset and time it with your ritual. Light a sparkler and dance or run around like you did when you were a child. Stay out all night and enjoy the magic.

LUGHNASADH: Bake a loaf of bread in the shape of sheaves of wheat or an animal. Break the bread and offer it back to the land, eating some yourself and sharing in the magic. Walk the land as part of the ritual, finding fields of wheat and barley that are just about to be harvested or are in the process of or have just been harvested. Give some of your bread there in offering as well as in gratitude.

MABON: Time your ritual with the sunset. Prepare some food from local produce to share with the land and the Fair Folk. Give thanks for the year's bounty and say some prayers for the sun, whose powers are diminishing. Welcome the growing darkness and honour the autumn season. Cut an apple in half sideways, revealing the five-pointed star within. Meditate upon the symbol.

• • •

These are just some examples of rituals that you can perform as a hedge witch. You are not limited to these, and you may find that you can create more rituals to work with your own landscape and in the otherworld. The sacred and the mundane will begin to overlap more and more in your life, and with each ritual you will find the liminal spaces in between, where you realise that the mundane is the sacred and vice versa. All of nature will begin to sing in your soul, and you will find a growing, deepening connection to it with each ritual act, offering, hedge riding, or spellcrafting that you create.

The midsummer sun beats down upon her shoulders. She stands in her garden, surrounded by the wildflowers that she sowed earlier in the spring. Butterflies and bees are all around her; pigeons are cooing in the beech tree overhead. The hawks are circling the skies, riding the thermals as the sun warms up the land, and the magpies chatter in the neighbour's trees. Around her all life is alive, vibrant, and strong. She feels that energy in her soul and raises a cup of mead to the skies in honour of the bees' blessings.

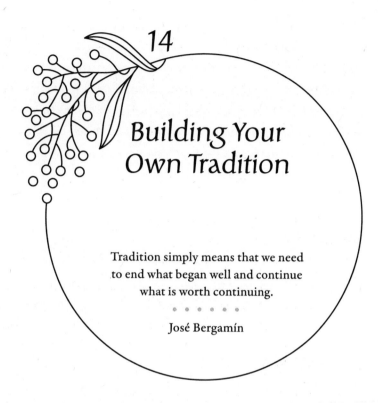

14

Building Your
Own Tradition

Tradition simply means that we need
to end what began well and continue
what is worth continuing.

• • • • • •

José Bergamín

Traditions give us a sense of security and stability. They can be wonderful aides to expression, giving us a solid foundation from which to work. They give us a sense of where we are going because we have confirmed what we are currently doing based upon a solid reflection of the past. In this book I have given you the information to begin creating your own hedge witch tradition, should you so wish. I haven't given you a singular tradition in and of itself because the Craft of a hedge witch is personal and individual. It will grow and change to meet the interests and needs of the individual practitioner. No two hedge witches will practice in the same way. The benefit of having your own personal tradition means that you have a reference, although that reference should be used to grow your own tradition and help you walk the path instead of becoming dogma and keeping you held within its bonds, never changing and never moving forwards. Traditions change, evolve, grow, and adapt for each hedge witch.

When a tradition becomes unwilling to adapt and evolve to meet modern criteria, it can lead to certain problems. A tradition that is not allowed to evolve and grow becomes dogma, which is anathema to modern Paganism. For example, just because something has always been done a certain way doesn't mean that it's the best way. Ancient Celtic druids used animal sacrifices, for instance, which is unacceptable today. They may even have committed human sacrifice, which we would find utterly abhorrent today. It may have been part of the practice then, but that doesn't mean that it has to be part of the practice now.

Kerr Cuhulain puts it very succinctly in his book *Wiccan Warrior*:

> Life involves change. And that change may make institutions and traditions obsolete. We shouldn't be doing things because they've always been done that way; the Warrior does things a particular way because that way brings results. If the traditional way didn't work anymore, the Warrior seeks alternatives.[42]

I've stated before that age does not equal validity. Just because a tradition is old doesn't make it more powerful or valid than a tradition that you created yesterday. What matters is authenticity. Is this tradition true to you? Does it allow you to be your own true, authentic self? In the past, many traditions within modern Paganism have suffered from a lot of claims of authenticity from other traditions, teachers, and lore that have since been found out to be false. They equated authenticity to something that was "old," equating the old with an air of power and authority. But we know that we need to keep evolving, learn new things, and experiment in order to grow and change. Within the context of modern Paganism and Hedge Witchcraft specifically, we need to be open to change and not allow ourselves and our practice to stagnate simply because it is "tradition." We need to acknowledge our sources and look them up carefully. We need

---

42 Cuhulain, *Wiccan Warrior*, 27.

to acknowledge that the founders of modern Paganism lifted some of the material from other people, sometimes with and sometimes without their permission. We have to acknowledge that some of the stuff was just made up to fill in gaps. Again, just because something has been "made up" recently does not invalid it in any way. If it works, then it works. Just know what you are doing and why and where it came from, either from yourself or from the experience or imagination of others.

Let's look at Gerald Gardner, for example. We have been able to piece together where he got the elements to form his own tradition. He did not create or discover a long-lost tradition of Witchcraft but created his own using what spoke to him and what worked for him, including elements that he was taught through his work with others in the Craft. His own personal interests in naturism (nonsexual nudity for health and well-being) led him to incorporate that within his tradition. We have no evidence to suggest that witches before him ever performed rituals in the nude. We have some woodcuts and such in the Middle Ages during the witch craze that depict naked women as witches, but these are more a reflection of the imagination and titillation of the artist rather than the truth.

Gardner did follow the witch's tradition of "if it works, use it." He took elements from the Egyptian pantheon and the names of Hebrew demons from medieval grimoires. From the medieval play *Le Miracle de Theophile* he created a popular Wiccan chant known as "Eko Eko Azarak" (which many modern Wiccans would probably be horrified to know that it was used by the character Salatin to conjure the devil[43]) and lifted rituals and specific tools (with or without permission, we just don't know) from Aleister Crowley's works. He incorporated Christian elements such as scourging (from the Christian Flagellants) and copied ritual elements lifted from *The Key of Solomon* such as the making of tools and their consecration, preparation and raising a magic circle, as well as including the tools of the athame and the bolline.[44] Even the term *Book of Shadows* may

43   de Givry, *Witchcraft, Magic and Alchemy*, 109.
44   Cuhulain, *Wiccan Warrior*, 34.

have been lifted by Gardner from an article that appeared in the *Occult Observer* in 1949.[45]

While it's all well and good to borrow (with respect) from other traditions, it is important to honour them and acknowledge where it came from, its history, and not to claim it as your own. Using Christian magic, chants to summon demons from texts and plays belonging to the Middle Ages, and poetry from Rudyard Kipling—as Gardner did in his Book of Shadows[46]—and then claiming it to be something that it is not is just not cool. Own your tradition. Acknowledge your sources. Put in your own stuff using your own talents. Respect other traditions, and do not dilute the truth of yours or any other modern Pagan tradition any further. Modern Paganism has suffered so much because of this dilution, the reiteration of now-disproved theories and historical accounts, that it is time to address and correct these errors and claims in order to speak and live our truths.

My own personal Book of Shadows (a book you make yourself that contains the written lore, rituals, spells, and everything else about your tradition) contains material and work by other witches. I have sourced and accredited all the information that I can and am not passing on this material as "ancient" or as a tradition that is hundreds of years old. It is also filled with my own poetry, chants, rituals, spells, and knowledge. We can learn so much from others, and that's a good thing. But we have to acknowledge our teachers and respect their work. For a good overview on the Book of Shadows, see *The Witch's Book of Shadows* by Jason Mankey.

All that being said, let's look at how we can build our own tradition.

How to Build Your Own Tradition

First, it is important to establish what it is that you want to achieve with your Craft. What do you want to work towards? What is your ultimate goal, remembering that your goals will shift and change, and therefore so will your tradition? At this point in time, what is it that you want to do

---

45 Ibid., 46.
46 Ibid., 36.

with your Craft? It's good to have this kind of objective, as it narrows your focus. Do you want to specialise in a certain area, such as herbcraft, working as a priest or priestess, or environmental, political, or social activism? If you're not quite sure yet of your goal, that's fine. List your interests instead, and then see if you can narrow it down to something achievable. There is no time frame; these may shift and change from year to year, and that's okay. You might even choose to study something different each and every year as part of your tradition. What's important is to define what is important to you right now.

Next, do your research. This book goes some way to helping you with information on the Craft, but you must read lots of books as a solitary practitioner of the Craft. Take courses if any are offered in your area. Some people are lucky enough to have public Witchcraft classes available; others might have peripheral classes on offer such as foraging, candle making, gardening, etc. Expand your knowledge; think laterally.

Once you feel confident that you know what the Craft is about (and don't forget that we never stop learning), then you can begin to write down how your own tradition is practised, should you so wish. Writing things down gives form to ideas; it solidifies them and allows you to look over your words and really define your terms. With your list of goals or interests, you can begin to create an outline of your tradition. You may turn this into your own personal Book of Shadows or simply keep the information in an easily accessible filing system for future reference.

Here are some things to think about:

- What holidays/festivals/seasons are you going to celebrate? When will you celebrate them: by the calendar or by nature? How will you do so with respect to your local environment? What can you glean from local lore to help you decide? How will you honour the moontides?

- What deities will you honour, if any?

- What tools will you use, if any?

- What clothing will you wear? Will it be ritual specific? Are street clothes acceptable or even preferred?

- What methods will you employ in ritual: What type of circle casting will you use, how will you call in the elements, etc.?

- What kinds of magic will you employ in your rites and rituals, if any? Will you have your own set list of magical symbols or use/borrow from other traditions? Will you create and/or adapt spells for your own use?

- How will you work your ethical code into your practice? Will you have a list of guidelines or rules?

- Will you have a written Book of Shadows for your tradition or more of a filing system for all your work that you can retrieve when you wish?

- How will you accredit things that are not your own?

- How open will you be regarding your Craft? Should they ask and should you be willing to divulge, how can you tell others what it is that you do in simple and easy to understand terms?

It can be helpful to create spreadsheets to link the information you have gleaned all together in one place. For instance, you can have a sabbat sheet with columns that state festival name, time of celebration, mythos, symbols, ritual actions, magical associations, spellcraft, offerings, etc. Fill in each one with regards to a sabbat and soon you'll have your own set of sabbat celebrations. You can do a similar one just for spellcraft, with columns that list need/goal, ingredients, elements used, ritual actions, symbols/magical associations, outcome, etc.

The next step is to actually do the work.
You've thought about it, you've researched it,
you've organised it; now it's time to live it.

Try out the festival celebrations over the course of a year. See what works and what doesn't. If certain things don't work or don't seem to work in conjunction with the rest of the seasonal celebrations, then change it. You might need to tweak things here and there for a year's cycle or more until you feel comfortable. You may prefer to write up completely new rituals each year. Taking the time to think about them in advance can help create a cohesive practice, even if you are improving each ritual. You will at least have a context to work with, and things will probably work more smoothly. You may like to improvise some aspects of the ritual and not others, such as how you call in the elements, depending on where you are holding the ritual. You may like to honour different deities from a pantheon at each sabbat or write a new poem or song at each full moon for the Goddess. Tradition doesn't mean that you have to do the exact same thing over and over again; it is a framework that you can use to be creative without straying too far from your original intention.

These are just a few of the things to think about when creating your own tradition. Remember the witchy motto: use what works. Be true to yourself, and you cannot go wrong.

She records the ritual that she has just performed, writing it down in her journal. She is pleased with how it turned out. It was personal and meaningful, and it felt like it was blessed by the wind in the trees, the moon overhead, and the badgers that came through the hedge to snuffle and wuffle around the trees. She is already thinking of how to expand upon this ritual to work with the energies created and write more, each one building upon the other to celebrate the cycle of the seasons and honour the Lord and Lady. With a contented sigh, she closes the book and stretches, her heart full and the inspiration flowing.

PART 4
Lore

*In this section, we look at elements of spellcraft,
herbcraft, and countryside lore and how they
can help us develop our own tradition.*

15

Spellcraft

Those who don't believe in
magic will never find it.

· · · · · ·

Roald Dahl,
The Minpins

The first thing that many people think of when they hear the word *Witch-craft* is magic. We all know that witches cast spells; we've grown up with this idea through fairy tales, television, movies, and popular fiction. But just what is magic, and how can you use it to create positive change in the world? What are the implications of using magic, and what are the ethics involved? How do you craft a spell? We'll look at all these ideas in this chapter, beginning with the simple ethics of doing no harm.

Do No Harm
(or the Least Amount of Harm)

As a hedge witch, I will always urge you to look and think about everything that you do, all the lore and material that you come across, for there are layers upon layers of meaning, intent, and history behind everything. You don't just want to parrot back quotes and sayings without truly knowing what lies behind them. Remember, the opinions of others may be important, but don't make them your opinions; you have your own voice, your own mind, and you will have to think very hard about what you do and say in your own practice in order to make it authentic to your true self.

All in all, what is probably the most important thing to remember is this: Witchcraft is a path that does not contain dogma. Therefore, any ethical code is to be used as a guideline, not as a rule or law that is set in stone. Far too often people turn wonderful stories and poetry into literal dogma, which is anathematic to Witchcraft. This happens in other spiritualties and religions the world over, to the detriment of all.

So here we find the witch version of the Golden Rule. Instead of "treat others as you would wish to be treated," it is often simply condensed into two words: "harm none." Again, though it is only two words, this is something that needs to be considered carefully because we cause harm to certain things and in certain situations every single day. Witches who are giving or undertaking radiation or chemotherapy will have a different take on this, as will witches who work in the garden and who understand pruning and/or disease control. Instead, it might be better to think about causing the least amount of harm in any given situation and in life in general.

Harming someone is something that is different for each person. You cannot define it for another person. For me, living with the least amount of harm means living organically as much as possible, being a vegetarian, and treating others with respect and kindness, just for starters. For others, it might mean living off-grid and going vegan. Still again, for some it might mean giving up the car and relying on public transport, doing interfaith work in the city, and promoting green spaces to bring inner-city communities together. It's often not enough to do the least amount of harm; we also should want to promote and encourage kindness, compassion, and harmony in all our relationships. Doing the least amount of harm is just the baseline from where we start our work, and then we expand that outwards as far as we can in our lives.

Still, there are other witches who do not follow the "harm none or do the least amount of harm" way of being. They see it as being within their personal freedom to heal or harm as they please. I personally feel that intentionally and maliciously harming others also harms ourselves. If we are the type of person who wants to harm another, we have some pretty nasty energy going on inside of ourselves. This energy is going to leak out into every aspect of our lives and spread like a poison. Does this mean that I'm all love and light? Of course not. People piss me off, politicians do stupid and reckless things, people on the street behave badly, strangers on social media may attack me. How I respond to all of this, however, is in a way that doesn't cause the harmful negativity to spread even further. I can stand up for myself, I can write to the politicians and march in the streets, I can realise that I have no control over how other people act—that's their responsibility—as I choose my own battles. I act with kindness and compassion as much as I can, and I can stand strong in my beliefs when needed. The two are not necessarily opposed.

Hedge witches have their own ethics, based upon their experiences and knowledge, and acknowledge that all actions have consequences. You may incorporate the harm none/do the least amount of harm concept into your ethics or not. However, in my opinion, it is something to think about, whether you are a witch or not.

What Is Magic?

Often you will see the word *magic* spelled with a "k" ("magick") in many modern books on Witchcraft. Some people use this spelling (pun intended?) to differentiate between the sleight of hand and stage tricks that performing magicians use and the magic that is found in the Old Ways. For myself, I never felt the need to differentiate this through spelling, as it's pretty obvious which is which, in my opinion. But it is out there, so if you do come across it, don't worry; we're talking about the same thing!

Magic is the use of natural forces to create change. It is really that simple. The powers found in the natural world are all forms of energy, just like we are. Some are simply denser in form than others. This energy can be used to change and shift certain patterns in order to bring about a more favourable outcome. There is a huge body of lore that comes with it, relating to all sorts of correspondences that teach us which herb heals what condition, which colour candle works best for certain spells, or what day of the week is most propitious for our work. Here I will cover the simple basics, for in Hedge Witchcraft we like to keep it simple. We work with what we have to hand and don't need to go searching in ancient grimoires for rare ingredients or use strange-sounding incantations in unknown languages (unless we really want to). The herbs we use are those that we find in the hedgerows or grow in our gardens or our windowsills (we will look at hedgerow herbs in chapter 16). The tools, as we've previously seen, are practical and are things found around the home. The words we use are in a language that is uncomplicated, and our understanding of how nature works in our environment forms the correspondences that we need in order to work our Craft.

What Is a Spell?

A spell is like a mini ritual or rite where we use the forces of nature to change or alter a situation. Like a ritual, it has a beginning, middle, and end. A spell differs from a prayer or petition to the gods in that we are working the magic ourselves and not leaving it to a higher power. That being said, invoking the deities that you work with to help with your spell isn't a bad idea, for they can certainly boost the potency if you have a good relationship with them! The Fair Folk can also bless your spellcraft, and if you have done a hedge riding to meet with your fairy companion, then they can advise you on creating and crafting your own spells, what to use, and what areas of research are required for what you need.

Spells usually use certain ingredients that correspond to the energy that you wish to work with, invoke, or get rid of in your work. That being said, some spells don't require anything but your mind. The complexity of a spell does not make it more effective. Often the simpler the spell is to create and cast, the better the results, in my own personal experience. Occasionally you may find that you need or desire to go for the gusto, and then you can elaborate a little in your practice. Let's look at some basic correspondences to get you going, but please be aware this is a very simplified list, and you can certainly expand through a little research. Using correspondences helps your spell to work more fluidly, going with the forces and powers of the natural world rather than working against them.

Days of the Week

Some days of the week have associations with different deities, and that energy can be used when crafting a spell. Our English words for the days of the week contain the names of Norse/Germanic deities and give us an idea as to their correspondences. The romantic languages such as French use Roman deities, though some magical traditions superimpose the Roman deities over the English names.

SUNDAY relates to Sunna, a solar deity, and is a day for working spells of increase during the light half of the year and decrease in the dark half of the year. It's also a good day to shed some light on certain issues.

MONDAY is the moon's day, from the god Mani, and is a good time to work with changing perspective and emotions, the tides of our lives, and also performing divination.

TUESDAY is Tyr's day, a god of honour, justice, and the battle for what is right and true, and so is a good day for legal disputes, personal integrity, and working your will.

WEDNESDAY is Woden's day, a day for working with divination, the runes, and for winning battles and gaining strength.

THURSDAY is Thor's day, a day to work spells for victory over negativity, fight for the good of all, and bring rain, storms, and fertility to the crops.

FRIDAY is Freya's day, another good day to work fertility magic, increase self-love and worth, and perform divination and really magic of all kinds, for Freya is a goddess of magic and Witchcraft.

SATURDAY is Saturn's day, a remnant of our Roman past that
strangely enough never translated into an English form. This is
a day for turning away negativity and doing banishing spells of
all kinds.

Times of Day

The different times of day are useful in spellcasting, as they each have
their own energy:

DAWN is great for new beginnings or to gain inspiration.

NOON is a good time for gaining strength and power.

SUNSET is good for the endings of things and also for healing.

MIDNIGHT, also known as the witching hour, is a good time to
magically boost any spell.

Colours

Using colour to correspond to what you want to achieve has been used
for millennia. Coats of arms, fashion, and décor, for instance, all use colour
in order to effect a response. Here is a basic list of colour correspondences,
though you may find that some colours have a different or deeper and more
personal meaning to you, in which case, go with it!

WHITE: Purity, honesty, truth; white is also an all-purpose
colour if you don't have any other colours to hand

YELLOW: Inspiration, creativity, new beginnings, travel

ORANGE: Courage, strength, optimism, luck, fortitude

PINK: Love, luck, relationships

RED: Passion, love, strength, power, courage

PURPLE: Power, higher consciousness, status

BLUE: Healing, emotion, calm

GREEN: Abundance, wealth, prosperity, fairy energy, fertility

Brown: Grounding, animals, fertility

Black: Banishing, grounding

Numbers

Numbers sometimes play a part in magical traditions, so here are some of the basic numerical correspondences:

1: Universal life force

2: The Goddess and the God, duality and polarity

3: Longstanding magical number, lucky number, number of the Goddess

4: The elements, seasons, four directions of north, south, east, and west

5: The elements (including spirit), the pentagram or pentacle

6: A number related to the God and masculine solar energy

7: A number related to the Goddess and feminine lunar energy

8: The number of sabbats, also abundance and infinity

9: Extra-powerful magical number, as it is 3 × 3

0: Potential, stillness, nonbeing

13: A lucky/unlucky number for some people; also the number of full moons in a year

• • •

We have already looked at some correspondences in relation to the deities and the elements previously in this book. There are many, many others that you will come across or make associations with on your own. Please remember that just because someone uses an orange candle in a spell to bring luck into their lives doesn't mean that it will work for you, especially if you do not associate orange with luck or if it just doesn't feel right.

Go with what works for you because your own personal symbology will have much more meaning than that devised by someone else. The above are simply given as guides that many people seem able to agree upon.

Let's now take a look at how to craft a spell, and then I'll give some examples of spells that you can use or from which you can gain inspiration to create your own.

How to Craft a Spell

As mentioned previously, a spell has a beginning, a middle, and an end. Let's start at the beginning!

1. A spell must first begin with a clear intention. This is perhaps the most important part of a spell. An intention that is unclear will not manifest clearly, if at all.

2. Find out what correspondences will work. These will lend their energies to your spell, allowing you to work with the flow of the natural world. How will the energy that you raise be released through the correspondences you have chosen? Are you going with elemental correspondences? Combining it with others? This is important to think about and remember when spellcasting.

3. You will need to have all the ingredients to hand before casting. This includes a host of little things that are often forgotten, such as matches for lighting candles or a pen to write down the spell or intention, etc.

4. Ground and centre, meditate, or do what you have to do to enter the work in a good frame of mind. Some spells work well with high emotion but can lack clarity. Be focused above all else.

The middle part of a spell is the actual working itself. This consists of:

5. Setting up any spell ingredients in the correct manner.

6. Raising energy and power: you can use energy from the earth, the sea, the sky, and even your own personal energy. Do not deplete your own personal energy in a spell; always try to combine it with other energy so that you have enough afterwards to reap the rewards.

7. Sending the energy in whatever form you have chosen for the spell. This might include charging an object, filling it with energy, and then releasing that energy using one of the elements; for example, filling a stone with the energy and intention of your spell and then casting it into a river.

Finally, we have the conclusion of the spell, which consists of:

8. Grounding any excess energy so that it doesn't affect you while you wait for the spell's manifestation. Send any excess energy back into the earth, eat and drink something, and relax for a few minutes.

9. Putting everything away (this means keeping your things in good order so that when you do your next spell you will always know where things are and have clean tools, etc.).

10. Write down exactly how you did the spell in every little detail. Sometimes spells simply don't work, and having your records in good order might mean that you can double-check your work. It might be a simple thing that needs tweaking or a complete rewrite. Often what doesn't work is our greatest teacher.

11. Allow the spell to do its work. This means that you do not constantly check on the status of a spell but rather trust in the energies that you have raised and sent out to do their work. Some spells take hours or days to manifest; some weeks, months, or years. You can try to set a time limit on your spellcrafting, but this can be a boon or a hindrance.

Spellcrafting works with the powers of nature; forcing nature, rather than working with it, will not manifest in something positive.

12. Be open to the results. Sometimes the powers of nature will manifest your intention in ways that you never thought of, so be open and aware to what comes into your life or how things have changed in every possible way that you are able.

Spell Ingredients

Spell ingredients that are easily to hand and that you know personally are the best to use. Forget "eye of newt" and suchlike: work with everyday things you come across in the natural world.

For instance, here is a list of things you may find in your daily life:

CAT'S WHISKERS. I have two cats, and they shed a whisker or two from time to time. These can be collected and used for spells to increase grace, stealth, beauty, and, above all else, perception. Never, ever cut a cat's whisker from its face. Wait until they shed them naturally.

CAT'S CLAW SHEATHS. Again, these are shed naturally and look just like little claws that have been hollowed out. These are great for protection magic, especially in self-defense. Once again, only take ones that have been shed naturally.

BIRD'S FEATHERS. I find feathers in my garden and on my daily walks everywhere I go, whether in a city or out in the countryside. Different bird's feathers can have different correspondences. For instance, pigeon feathers are abundant and can be used for spells of abundance, adaptability, and perseverance. Crow feathers can be used for spells to gain intelligence or for cunning craft. Jay feathers are great for self-confidence and glamour magic, as are magpie feathers. There is a major caveat when it comes to taking home wild bird feathers or anything from the wild, however. Different countries have different laws defining what you are and aren't allowed to collect from the wild, so please do ensure you check this first before you collect anything from the wild, whether it is feathers, plants, stones, etc. Some species of plant or animal, or stones from a river, beach, or other sites might be protected. This means doing some homework first!

BONES. Again, see the caveat above. You are safe with bones from meat that you have eaten. In the wild, I've found whole crow skulls, deer skulls, rabbit skulls, leg bones of rabbit and deer, and even entire wings of pheasants who fell prey to a fox. I have checked to see whether these items are legal in my area to take. In England we have the Wildlife and Countryside Act to guide us, with not a few species that are afforded extra protection. You will have to be careful about what you collect when it comes to bones you may find in the wild through death only by natural causes. Some animals who died through a car collision may not be collected, such as otters in England, for example. All that being said, if collected legally, bones are wonderful tools for spellcrafting as well as for your altar if you personally connect with the animal and have obtained them lawfully.

STONES. There is an abundance of flint and quartz where I live. On the beach I can find carnelian and, if I'm supremely lucky, amber. Using local stones is so much better than buying semi-precious stones that have been blasted out of the earth with explosives and even sometimes treated with chemicals or radiation to make them change colour. Check whether you are allowed to collect stones from a site beforehand.

EGGSHELLS. These can be ground up into a powder and used in spells for fertility, abundance, and protection.

Snail Shells. I come across empty snail shells almost every time I do some gardening. These are great for protection magic, as well as for magic for the hearth and home.

Houseplants. Everyday houseplants can be used in your spellcrafting. Spider plants are great for spells of strength, perseverance, and abundance. Cacti are great for protection. Peace lilies can be used for—you guessed it: peace!

• • •

This is just a small sample of everyday things you might come across that you can use in your spellcraft.

Be creative and have an open mind when you are working on the construction of your spell; you may find you have everything that you need right at your fingertips.

Let's now turn our attention to some spells that I have created and that have been tried and tested in my own work. These can be used as they are or taken as examples as to how you can create your own spells. Personalising any spell is, in my opinion, what will really make it work. The ingredients used here are those that are particular to my location, so you may have to adjust to what you have in your home environment. Be open, be creative, and be clear as to what you want to achieve.

Spell for Healing

This is a spell to help someone overcome a major illness. This spell was written to decrease a disease for someone, so the first day of this spell is on a full moon to utilise its power, and then every night for a week afterwards to use the waning energy to help decrease the disease. There was also an eclipse that first night, so I used those energies as well. The elemental correspondences for this spell are fire and earth.

For this spell, you will need:

- A seven-day jar candle (white)

- A plate

- Sandalwood oil diluted with a carrier oil

- Herbs (I used ivy for health, rosemary for purification, and apple branches cut into small pieces for health and longevity)

Call into yourself the powers of the full moon, drawing them into you. Then pull up earth energy into your body and mix the two together. Charge the herbs with that energy. Either write the person's name on the glass jar of the candle or inscribe a healing symbol or rune that is personal to you and the situation on the exposed wax. Anoint the top of the candle with the diluted sandalwood oil, rubbing it on and avoiding the wick. You can also rub the oil on the exterior of the glass jar, if you so wish. Next, bring in more energy and charge the white candle with that energy, letting it flow from your hands into the candle. Sprinkle the herbs in a circle around the base of the candle clockwise; it's good to have the candle on a plate for this.

Call to the deities and say a prayer for the person's health. Alternatively, you could say a chant like:

> *(Name of person), I send healing to thee*
> *That health is now restored to thee*
> *By apple, rosemary, sandalwood, and ivy*
> *By sigil and fire, so may it be!*

Light the candle and see the energy flowing up from the herbs and lighting up the healing symbol or the person's name that you carved onto the candle. See the candle glowing with energy and that energy being released through the flame out into the world, directed towards the recipient. See them healed and whole, enjoying life to the fullest. Concentrate on this for as long as you can, and then you can either let the candle burn all the way out or put it out and relight it every night for seven nights afterwards.

If you need to leave the candle burning for a short amount of time but cannot be in the same room, place it in a fireplace or the bathtub or shower (away from shower curtains) and close the door so no pets can come in and investigate. Let the magic flow. Ideally, never leave a burning candle unattended.

A Binding Spell

When you are in a situation where you feel threatened or have suffered abuse or discomfort from a person, then you can always perform a binding spell. This spell binds the bad behaviour, but it does come with a caveat: what you do unto others can also be done to you. So think clearly about the essential need for this spell: use it if it is necessary, not just for kicks. If you are suffering mental or physical abuse, please do seek the help of the authorities and those in the medical profession. This spell may be performed at any time; however, during a dark moon or at the witching hour will add extra boosts.

For this spell, you will need:

- Paper and pen
- Red or black thread

Draw a picture of the object to be bound, whether it is a person or an object. You can also use a person's full name or even a photograph if you have one. If it is a person, visualise that person unable to harm you in any way, maybe by having a brick wall between you both or seeing their words or actions bouncing off a crystalline bubble that surrounds and protects you. Say the following words as you wrap the thread nine times around the object, binding it.

> *I bind you, (name of person)*
> *From doing harm to me*
> *By the power of three times three*
> *(Name of person), bound art thee*
> *This is my will, so mote it be!*

Keep the materials in a safe place or bury them. You can always reverse this spell, should you need to, by untying the cord from the object, unless you buried it and it has decomposed.

The Witch's Ladder Spell

This is an old traditional charm that can be used for any purpose, whether it be protection, healing, binding, money, love (ensure that you are not thinking of a specific person here; instead, visualise yourself as being worthy of love), or drawing anything you need to you. You will need to collect nine symbols of what you wish to achieve with this spell. Feathers, herbs, holed stones—anything that works with the energies you are calling in. Have a long cord or piece of twine or even wool and ensure that it is at least three feet long. You will tie each symbol into the cord while reciting this chant and visualising your desired outcome:

> *By knot of one the spell's begun*
> *By knot of two it will come true*
> *By knot of three this thing I see*
> *By knot of four 'tis through the door*
> *By knot of five my spell will thrive*
> *By knot of six this thing I fix*
> *By knot of seven on earth be heaven*
> *By knot of eight I rule my fate*
> *By knot of nine this thing be mine*

Hang the "ladder" in a prominent place in your home: a sunny window is ideal. Let the magic be sent out, and enjoy the results!

Spell for Cleansing and Protection

This was originally used to restore the energy to my back garden after someone had defiled it.

This spell is a powerful one. It calls upon the Celtic goddess Andraste. She was the goddess that Boudicca called upon before she went out and kicked some Roman butt. Andraste is a goddess that is particularly suited to women who have suffered at the hands of men or for anyone who has suffered grave injustices. I would not call on her for trivial matters. Boudicca called on her "as a woman to a woman" to exact her revenge on those who beat her, raped her daughters, and stole her wealth, and to bring back control of their land into their own hands. Andraste is a very powerful deity of the land, particularly here in East Anglia. I also invoke Boudicca's spirit and legacy. The goddess Brighid is also called upon for healing in this spell. After cleansing an area of energy, it's always good to fill that void with something. Here, it was filled with protection through Andraste and Boudicca, and healing through Brighid. You might note that the magic number of three is present in the goddesses/spirits called.

For this spell, you will need:

- Incense: any herb or incense that has protective qualities is good; I used Star Child's purification and also their protection incense for this rite.[47] (As it was performed outdoors, my asthma wasn't affected.) You can also burn a single protective herb, such as oak bark, on a small charcoal disc used for incense. Birch bark can be used as purification. The incense/herbs represent the elements of air and fire.

- Water and salt, representing the elements of earth and water. This will be used to purify the area. (My garden is okay with a bit of saltwater, as I live next to the sea. If you are in an area where saltwater will hurt the plants, place a stone in the water instead to bring together the powers of earth and water.)

- Knife or staff or some other item that is also a weapon (a sharp kitchen knife will do if you don't have anything else; I used my working knife that I bought in an outdoor/hunting shop in Sweden for when I am out camping). It will be used to cast the circle. I don't normally use a knife in my circle

47 See https://starchild.co.uk/.

castings, but for this spell I felt the energy of a weapon was necessary. You might disagree, in which case use whatever feels right for you.

- Stang or wand

- A bell or some other item that has a clear ringing sound to drive away negative energy. You can even use pots and pans and a wooden spoon to strike them with! I used a "bell branch" that I made for my druid rites, which is an apple branch that has nine silver bells attached to it with ribbons of black, red, and white to represent the otherworld.

- Three stones; local stones are best. I used flint, quartz, and carnelian, all of which are found locally. These stones will be used as ward stones.

- An offering

This spell can be timed to correspond with astrological/astronomical phenomena. I performed this spell on a Thursday, which is a good day for spells of power, strength, battles, and justice. This was done just shortly after noon, so I also called down upon the power of the sun to aid me in this work. If the timing you prefer is at night, you can call upon the stars and moon or even the power of the dark moon to aid you in your work. To calculate timings in greater detail, perhaps using astrological and/or astronomical timings, you can use an ephemeris, which is available quite widely. There are also lots of books available that will teach you more about the detailed correspondences and timings.

CASTING THE SPELL

Cast the circle to the boundary limits with the knife. Invoke the spirits of the land around you, the trees and grass, the birds and beasts, the clouds overhead, etc. Call to the four quarters to aid you in this spellcrafting ritual. Invoke the Lord and Lady.

Bless the items that are to be used in this ritual (incense, water, salt, bell, stones). For the water and salt, you can hold them up to the sky or hold your hand over them and feel the energies of the God or Goddess blessing them through you. You may say something like:

I bless this salt through the power of the God.
I bless this water through the power of the
Goddess. May they be fit for my work.

For the other items such as the bell and stones, you can then bless them by using the four elements: sprinkling of salt for earth, then water, and then pass them through the incense smoke for fire and air. As you do each item, say:

I bless this by the elements of earth,
water, air, and fire. So may it be.

Then speak words of intention, which are to cleanse and purify the area of any energy you wish to banish. Use words that come from the heart; it doesn't have to be grand or fancy. Meaningful words are much more effective than grand poetry that is hollow.

Pick up the smouldering purification incense and walk widdershins (counterclockwise) around the circle. Cover as much ground as possible with the incense, especially if there are areas that have specifically been desecrated or have high volumes of negative energy. Do the same with the bell, visualising the sound blasting away all the energy that shouldn't be there. Place a pinch of salt in the water (or take up the water with a stone in it) and sprinkle the water around the area, seeing it cleansing the area.

Stand in the centre and draw energy down from the sun (or whatever heavenly body corresponds with the timing of your ritual spellcrafting). Fill yourself with this energy, then send it out through your stang/wand into the space while turning widdershins. Fill the space with this purifying energy, asking the spirits of the land around you and the Fair Folk to aid you in your work. Restore the rightful energy to the space.

Next take up the protection incense and walk the boundary of the area, this time deosil (clockwise), filling the area with the smoke. Really visualise the area benefitting from the smoke and energy of the herbs and resins being used, getting into every part of the area.

Stand in the centre of the area and invoke the goddess Andraste. Ask her to help ward and protect the space. Call to Boudicca to help you restore the desecration of the area. Again, use words from the heart.

Take up the knife and now cast a warding/protective circle of energy deosil out to the boundary of the area. Use your own personal energy combined with that of Andraste and Boudicca, casting it forth as you turn clockwise around the area.

Afterwards, draw into yourself more divine energy from Boudicca and Andraste, as well as earth energy from beneath your feet. When you feel yourself brimming with energy, pour it into the three stones. Then bury the stones in the centre of the space, knowing that they are doing their work. You may say something like:

> *Flint, quartz, and carnelian stone,*
> *protect this hearth and this home.*
> *By the power of the three, this is my will; so may it be.*

Stand or sit for a moment, seeing the warding settling into place. Call upon the goddess Brighid for healing as you place your hands upon the ground. Feel the healing energy flow through you and into the space. Thank the deities and then give the offering. Close down the spellcrafting ritual and know that your work is done. You can renew this warding every year on the anniversary of this date, should you so wish and if you feel it is necessary.

• • •

After I had performed this spell, it felt like the area was "mine" again, that space of my back garden that had been desecrated. When I began the ritual, the sky was blue and there wasn't a cloud in sight. However, when I called upon Andraste, the sun went behind a cloud, the only one in the sky. I could feel her dark energy seeping into myself and the land, powerful and strengthening—and a little frightening, all that power. I could feel the strength of spirit from Boudicca and see it reflected in the land around me. Brighid's healing filled in the last gap in my wounded soul and area, and the balance was restored. As I sat afterwards and rested, a deer came through the hedge, followed by a pheasant. The spirits of the land were pleased.

· · ·

The above are just a few examples of what you can do with magic. In spell-crafting it is important that what you do resonates with *you*. Don't just copy someone else's spell unless it fits perfectly with what you feel is right in your own work. As a hedge witch, you have to think for yourself and do your homework. You will have to learn the associations and correspondences that have meaning in your own locality. You will have to learn the times and tides of your local area, as well as those of your own body and soul. Performing spells when some of these are out of sync means that there is that extra barrier that your magic may have to get through. If you are tired or sick, then perhaps it is not the best time for spellcasting, unless it is a healing spell for yourself (combined with taking any medications necessary).

> *Magic is not a cure-all. It is something*
> *that is our birthright, but it should be*
> *honoured for the very special energy and*
> *ability that it is—and be used wisely.*

*S*he could feel the magic all around her, the circle buzzing with the energies raised towards her goal. She released those energies with the final words of her spell and knew that they were winging their way up into the air and eastward towards the desired destination. She stood, gathered up any stray energy into her body, and helped direct that, sending it with the rest of the energy flowing outwards. When all the energy had been sent, she exhaled long and slow and sank to her knees on the dew-wet grass. There was still some extra energy within her, so she released this back into the earth with a prayer of thanks. She then lifted her hands and washed her face with the dew, reviving and refreshing her after her work. She smiled and looked at the full moon, knowing that her spell had worked.

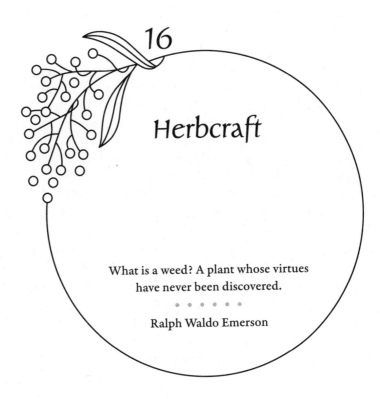

16

Herbcraft

What is a weed? A plant whose virtues
have never been discovered.

· · · · · · ·

Ralph Waldo Emerson

In this chapter we will look at herbs that can be used both medicinally
and magically. All of these can be found in the hedgerows here in Britain.
You may find similar herbs in your area that you can research and incorporate into your own Craft. You may also live in a completely different
environment to where I live, so you may want to research the herbs and
herbcraft from your local area. I strongly recommend working with a qualified herbal practitioner first and foremost.

Before using any herbs, please ensure that you know exactly what they
are and where they came from; pollutants are a very real thing even in rural
areas. Some harmful herbicides can linger in root systems or contaminate
the soil, even if everything looks lovely, wild, and pristine. I have not
included dosage information for any of the herbs listed in this book
for a very good reason. You will need to consult a medical or master

herbalist in order to find the right dosage for your own specific needs, as these vary from person to person and are entirely dependent upon your own physical and mental health, whether you are on any medication or have any medical conditions that may contraindicate with any herbs. Do not take any herb internally without qualified supervision; doing so may seriously harm your health or even prove fatal. Magically, you will need to ensure that the herbs are safe to use; when in contact with your skin, for instance, or if burned, find out if they produce toxic or dangerous fumes. Herbs are powerful things.

This is just a sample of what you may find growing wild in the hedgerows. But it's not the use of the herb that is important. What is most important is that you truly come to know and understand the herb as an ally, friend, and companion in your journey through life. Here are some of my favourites.

Nettle
(Urtica dioica)

Nettles are probably best known for their sting, though not all species sting. The sting comes from tiny hairs found all over the plant that pierce the skin and release an acid, which causes the sting. For hours afterwards you may feel this fading and then returning. You can combat the sting straightaway if you have some burdock nearby; crush a leaf and rub on the sting. It helps somewhat, but I've found it doesn't take it away completely.

Stinging aside, nettles are a wonderful plant. They are just so useful and beneficial to humans. In the spring they are particularly potent. The young leaves can be picked and made into a number of delicious foods, and the whole plant can be used to treat ailments of all kinds. They are also very useful in textiles, as they can be made into cloth, paper, and rope, as well as being a lovely dyeing agent. Nettles, like comfrey, are also beneficial to use in the garden as a fertiliser. Cut and soak in a covered bucket of water for a couple of weeks, let it get stinky, and then pour over the soil in the garden.

You just can't beat nettles for their benefits. They are chock-full of vitamins and minerals, especially iron—which, if you're vegetarian like me, is so essential. Nettles are also great if you suffer from anaemia. It is full of vitamin C, so when suffering from colds and flu, it's a great tonic to help you get back to health (or to prevent you from getting sick in the first place). It is high in calcium and vitamin K. Nettles boost the immune system, reduce blood sugar, and are also a diuretic, which is great if you suffer from fluid retention. If you have high blood pressure, nettle's properties can help reduce blood pressure. Nettles are also a galactagogue in that they increase breast milk production as well as supply new mothers and babies with a much-needed vitamin and immune system boost.

Nettles are known as blood purifiers as they help and support healthy kidney function. They are also known for helping those who suffer from arthritis (always use fresh herb for arthritis). A tincture made with apple cider vinegar or alcohol treats the condition, or you can just drink several cups of tea when it flares up. Nettles are also a great hair rinse!

The young leaves at the top of the plant are the ones that are used in your lotions and potions, teas and soups. Harvest the leaves before the plant flowers; after flowering, leave it alone as it can cause stomach upsets. It's also nice to give it a break after it's been helping you for months! After it flowers, you can also use the seeds; collect and dry them, then grind them and mix with honey to create a paste that is good for coughs. The roots can also be used and are harvested in the autumn. You can make a tincture with the roots. Studies have also found that nettle can help men with enlarged prostates.[48] Nettles also boost other herbs that have antihistamine qualities, so it's perfect for allergies and treating seasonal asthma when used in conjunction with herbs such as plantain.

So, before using the leaves, how to get rid of the sting? Some people are able to take the young leaves, roll them into tubes, and crush the little hairs/stingers before popping them into the mouth and eating them straight up. My herbal teacher was able to pick the leaves straight off the plant without getting stung, but I never developed that knack. So, in order to not get stung in the first place, cut the tops off with some scissors and let

48 Seal, *Hedgerow Medicine*.

them fall into a small basket. That way you don't have to touch the plant at all and can avoid the sting.

Next, boiling the leaves will eliminate the sting. It only needs a few minutes to boil before the sting is gone, so you can throw a handful into a teapot and let it steep for a bit before drinking. The lovely green taste of the first batch of nettle tea in the spring is so wonderful! I've found that using dried nettles just doesn't taste the same as the fresh herb. The dried herb can be a little bitter, whereas the fresh herb just tastes like the colour green, much like the smell of cut grass smells like the colour green. Am I getting a bit weird? Well, it's because nettles are full of chlorophyll, so there is some sense in my nonsense...

Nettle soup is fab: simply cut up an onion, a little bit of garlic (wild garlic, or ramsons, is perfect, and in parts of North America you can use wild leek or wild ramps), add as many nettles as you like (a lot!), and let it simmer. It will wilt like spinach. Then add water and boil it down, adding some sea salt. Blitz it with a hand blender and you've got a lovely rich green soup that is just calling out for hunks of bread to be dipped and savoured. Nettles were also used to make beer.

Nettles can be found everywhere in the UK. They are a true hedgerow plant, growing along many waysides, boundaries, and markers. Their ability to both help and harm gives them a real connection to the witches of ye olden times. You have to work carefully with nettle out of respect for its powerful properties. It's easy to grow as well: simply scatter some seeds in a small patch at the bottom of the garden, and you'll have your own supply near to hand whenever you wish to work with it. Cut it back before it self-seeds. You'll be able to cut it back several times before the last seeding at the end of summer, and then you can collect the seeds before the final cut. Save some for your work, sprinkle the rest onto the ground, and wait for the new shoots to tell you that spring has finally arrived!

Magically, nettle is a great herb for use in protection spells of all kinds. Here you can use both the fresh and dried versions. It is an herb that is connected to Ostara, as that is when it really makes its first appearance.

It is connected to the element of fire. It can be used to overcome fear. The infusion or tea can be used to purify and consecrate your tools. It is great for working with confidence and issues concerning respect. Finally, nettle is the primary herb to use in any problem with boundaries.

Nettle is a true ally for the witch. For me,
this is probably the number one herb to get
to know and work with in your Craft.

Dandelion
(Taraxacum officinale)

Perhaps one of the great stalwarts of herbalism next to nettle is dandelion. This fantastic plant has so many beneficial uses for both humans and non-humans. In the spring they are especially important to the pollinators who have woken up from their winter slumber are searching amongst the scarce blooms to feed. Please leave your spring dandelions as they are, even if they are in the middle of a manicured lawn! While later on in the year they can be a bit of a nuisance if you enjoy a pristine lawn, you may find that your feelings toward them turn when you discover just how beneficial these weeds truly are. In fact, it's said that the Victorians used to pull up the grass to allow the dandelions to grow![49]

Dandelion comes from the French *dent-de-lion,* or lion's tooth. Why? Well, the leaves are toothed, so a correlation was made, probably from someone who really likes lions! (Us cat lovers, we are everywhere.) This powerful herb is connected to the sun in that it opens and closes with sunlight. The whole plant is beneficial, from the flower to the root. It is becoming more popular to cook with the leaves of the dandelion plant, but it is mostly used fresh in salads. Some supermarkets even sell dandelion leaves! It is high in potassium and vitamin D, which is perfect for use as

49 Chamberlain, *Wicca Herbal Magic.*

a spring tonic. It helps liver function as well as acts as a purifier by stimulating the kidneys and bowels. It treats gallstones, urinary tract infections, menstrual disorders, and menopausal symptoms.

The root can be roasted and used as a coffee substitute. Dandelion is a diuretic, so if you are using this herb, you will find that you will need to visit the loo more often than usual. Its potassium-rich content counters the loss of the mineral through increased urination. It's great for fluid retention. The flowers can relieve headaches (simply pick one and chew it straight) or be made into beer or even dandelion wine. You can make a lovely salad dressing by infusing olive oil with dandelion flowers for a couple of weeks. The leaves can be used as a tea to promote good sleep, relieve indigestion, and also act as a febrifuge (to lower a fever). It's also been used to treat gout. When using the leaves, use the young leaves, as they are less bitter. Pick them in the spring and summer, usually up until the summer solstice. After that they may get too bitter to use, depending on your area. If you are regularly mowing the dandelions in your lawn, however, you will get a new crop every other week coming up with fresh leaves and flowers waiting to be used.

The sap from the plant was said to cure warts. Cut a stem, squeeze the juice onto the affected area, and let it dry. It will go a brownish colour; leave it on and don't wash it off. Repeat until the wart has gone away. There are charms that can be said as you do this, such as "Wart, begone; leave me alone." In fact, dandelion is good for treating many skin ailments, such as acne. It helps fight viral infections and also lowers blood pressure.

You can make a tincture from dandelion leaves,
flowers, and root, or a decoction from just the root.
This can be taken daily to help with arthritis,
constipation, eczema, acne and other skin
problems, fluid retention, and even hangovers!

Spiritually, dandelion can be used to cross over into the otherworld in order to talk to nature spirits or the Fair Folk or contact the ancestors. Drinking dandelion wine in spring and summer rituals and sharing it with the Fair Folk is a great way to connect and establish a good relationship with them.

Dandelion is a plant of the sun and the element of fire. Use it in fire rituals and spellwork to give them an extra boost of solar and fire energy. It's a persistent, tenacious little herb. Use it to strengthen resolve, overcome obstacles, and thrive in a poor environment. It can bring a sunny disposition when you're feeling down and help heal the heart and the solar plexus area, filling it with solar energy.

Hawthorn
(Crataegus monogyna)

Perhaps the most magical herbal ally for the hedge witch is the hawthorn. It literally means "hedge thorn." This tree is often used in hedges, alongside blackthorn, to create boundaries between fields, keeping cattle fenced in while still allowing for the movement of smaller creatures to pass through. Hawthorn's other folk name is whitethorn. Many new hedgerows are being planted today to reinstate these wildlife corridors where they were dug out by landowners for industrial farming. Industrial farming has caused severe loss of topsoil in many areas, especially here in the east of England, where the wind and rain, if left unobstructed, can blow or wash the top inches of soil from a field straight off and usually directly into roadways, causing hazards. Wildlife cannot move safely through fields or have hiding spots away from both predators and combine harvesters. By reinstating these hedges, life is brought back in myriad forms to an area, increasing the biodiversity and therefore the health of an area. Sadly, we are only learning this too late, for many of the ancient hedges are now forever gone.

Hawthorn is a perfect ally for the art of hedge riding, the practice which lies at the heart of Hedge Witchcraft. It is a fairy tree and connects this world to the otherworld. Hawthorns have colours often associated with the otherworld: the white of the flowers, the red of the berries, and the dark branches that often appear black, especially when wet. Often hawthorns are gateways for the Other Crowd to pass in and out of our world, and equally so can we, especially at the most liminal times of the year such as the turning of the seasons, dawn and dusk, and most especially at Beltane, Samhain, and Midsummer. These fairy trees are often protected by the locals of an area, and it is extremely bad luck to cut one down. In Ireland roads have been diverted to avoid a hawthorn tree standing alone in a wide-open expanse. Lone hawthorn trees are especially thought to be gateways to the otherworld, as Thomas the Rhymer discovered when he met the Queen of Elfland underneath the boughs of the May (May bush is another name for hawthorn, as it usually flowers in May, around the time of Beltane or May Day).

> *You will also often find a hawthorn tree*
> *near or right next to a sacred spring or*
> *well as a guardian of this sacred place and*
> *another entrance to the otherworld.*

There is much more lore surrounding the hawthorn, including not taking a blossoming branch of this tree inside the home as you will also be inviting in the fairies, who may not have your best intentions in mind. A wand made from a hawthorn tree is extremely useful in Hedge Witchcraft, but you must first be totally and completely certain that you have the permission of the tree and the Fair Folk before you take even one twig from a live tree. The hawthorn is associated with the element of fire, though it also has water associations in relation to emotion and the heart.

For those who prefer to follow the rhythms of nature rather than the calendar, Beltane arrives when the hawthorn is in bloom, which may or may not fall on April 31/May 1. Some years it can be a month later than these dates; sometimes earlier. The flowering branches are often used to decorate maypoles, around which the dancers weave the cycles of life with their long streamers. Washing your face with the dew from a hawthorn on May Day/ Beltane will bring beauty, although pretty much any dew on that special morning is also said to have the same effect. If you sleep under a hawthorn tree on Beltane eve, you will most likely see the Fair Folk processing by in all their finery. Whether you join them or not is another matter ...

Medicinally, hawthorn is best known for its benefits to the cardiovascular system. Do not use this herb (or any other herb, for that matter) without qualified supervision! It is a herb for the heart. It strengthens the heart muscle. It balances blood pressure, whether low or high, and improves circulation around the body. The flowers, leaves, and berries are used in this medicine in the form of tinctures, syrups, or strong teas. It can treat angina as well as help with damage from alcohol abuse. Anyone who has a heart condition should most definitely talk to their doctor and a professional herbalist before taking hawthorn medicinally, as it can react to any medication that you are currently using and make you very ill (such as anyone using beta-blockers).

You will have to be patient when gathering hawthorn for herbal use, as the flowers and early leaves of spring are much improved if you also add the berries from the autumn. You can also make jellies from the berries, as they are very high in pectin, but be careful and remove all the seeds, for they contain cyanide. You can make a hawthorn blossom wine or cordial in the spring or combine the autumn berries (known as haws) with elder and blackberries for a deep, rich, luxurious wine. You can eat the early leaves from the hawthorn tree, which are quite delicious and have the strange colloquial name of "bread and butter." Perhaps it was because these early leaves were so beneficial to the body that they were the bread and butter not only of the body, but also the heart and soul? At any rate, keeping an eye out for the hawthorn, making friends with one, and learning all that you can from it will help you in your Craft immensely.

Blackthorn
(Prunus spinosa)

The blackthorn is another fairy tree. Where the hawthorn (sometimes known as the whitethorn) meets or grows next to a blackthorn, that is most definitely a portal to the otherworld and the fairy realm. It is probably the most-used hedging tree alongside the hawthorn because its very long, sharp spikes will stop cattle from passing through. Indeed, these spikes can be very harmful as they sometimes contain a form of bacteria on them which, if you get scratched, can result in a bad infection. Be careful around the blackthorn!

The wood of the blackthorn is very hard, so it is often used for walking sticks and also the Irish shillelagh. As such, it corresponds to the element of earth. It is a very hardy tree and can grow in the poorest of soils under the most extreme of conditions. In the spring you can distinguish the blackthorn from the hawthorn as the blackthorn flowers first, before the leaves come out, and the hawthorn only flowers after the leaves have come out. The autumn fruit on the blackthorn are known as sloes and are a very dark purple, almost black in colour, and can sometimes grow to the size of a small plum. They are extremely sour unless they have been frozen by a frost, in which case they become tolerable. Sloes are probably best known for creating sloe gin and are a very easy way to make a lovely liqueur. Make some room in a bottle of gin (you may have to drink it, if you can manage, wink wink), and then gather up some sloes. Freezing them first or gathering them after a frost will make your liqueur even sweeter. For a tangier one, pick the ripe sloes before a frost and gently prick each one before popping it into the bottle of gin. Add some sugar, depending on your preferred sweetness, and let it sit for a month to three months or even longer. Decant into a nice bottle, and there you have it: sloe gin. If you prepare your sloe gin in September or October, you will have some ready for drinking at Yuletide celebrations or to give as gifts.

The flowers are good for fevers when made as a tea, but beware, for they are also laxative! Do be aware when ingesting blackthorn, especially the seeds and leaves, for they contain traces of cyanide. Large quantities can be fatal, so it is critical to consult a medical or master herbalist in order to find the right dosage for your requirements.

Here in England, when the blackthorn flowers (anytime from January to April), we usually get a second dose of winter. Winds from the north and east ravage the land and remind us that we are not out the woods just yet. One year the "blackthorn winter" came really late, at around Beltane, which, when you are used to celebrating the beginning of the summer tide, is a bit of a shock!

As a faery tree, you have to be very careful if you are to use or cut a stick from the blackthorn, not only because of the thorns but because it is protected by a specific tribe of faery known as Lunantishees.

Always ask for permission, and never, ever cut a stick from it on Beltane eve or Samhain eve. A staff made of blackthorn will ward you against those who would harm you and may also grant you access to the otherworld, but it is a tree that must be worked with using the utmost respect.

Wild Rose
(Rosa canina)

Sometimes known as the dog rose, the wild rose is a beautiful herb found in hedgerows throughout Britain. It was also known as witch's briar: how perfect! We all know that roses are the flowers of love, but it is also a great herbal ally for the hedge witch.

This is truly a plant that looks beautiful in all seasons. The pink flowers in spring and summer are a joy, and in autumn and winter the bright red hips add colour to the hedgerows, as well as provide much-needed food for wildlife. Indeed, the rose hips are high in vitamin C and can be made into a syrup for coughs and colds and all manner of winter ailments. The flower petals can also be used to help support the immune system. Using the flowers and hips together reduces fevers, acts as a diuretic, and boosts your immunity. You can make a decoction of the hips as a tea (boiling them in a covered pot over a longer period of time than you would for making a normal tea with the leaves) that can also help with cold and flu symptoms. Rose hip jelly is delicious; there is nothing better on a scone, in my opinion. When using rose hips, do be careful to strain it well and remove all the seeds because they have tiny hairs on them that, if ingested, can cause stomach irritation and worse. Like many other plants from this family (such as apple), the seeds contain cyanide. Do not take internally without supervision or professional advice.

The wild rose is linked to the otherworld,
for it is said that the Fair Folk use the rose
hips to make themselves invisible.

In Germany the wild rose is linked to the devil, which shows that it was a powerful herbal ally for many female practitioners who were feared by the patriarchy.

Rose petals have been used for millennia in beauty products such as rose water or as a perfume. They have been used in love spells and are thought to have aphrodisiac properties. Wild rose is a herb of the water element. Use it magically to increase self-love and find the beauty within. Decorate your altar or your stang with a garland of the flowers in spring and summer, and with the hips in winter to honour your hedge tradition. And above all, be open to love!

Bramble/Blackberry
(Rubus fruticosus)

Around my little village in the autumn, you have be out early when the blackberries are ripe. Villagers keep a close eye on the nearest accessible bushes, and as soon as they are ready, they will be picked. It is a joy to eat the first blackberry of the season plucked straight from the hedgerow. It signals the arrival of autumn and of the jam and crumble-making season.

Blackberry is also known as bramble, which I think describes them perfectly. They do and will bramble anywhere they can, through hedges and trees, shooting out long tendrils that you don't notice until you catch your clothing on them. They wander everywhere, and if you get one in your garden, you will be hard put to get rid of it should you so wish. They are extremely persistent and can grow anywhere, and the only way to get shot of them is to dig the roots up entirely (not an easy task). Then you'll find that the birds poop the seeds out somewhere in your garden, and before you know it, you've got another bush growing...

The blackberry is probably the most familiar plant from the hedgerow. Even small children know the blackberry and eagerly await its season. The flowers are very pretty, but beware the thorns! Everyone who has been blackberry picking will usually come away with a scratch or three. But don't pick the blackberry after Michaelmas, or some say after Hallowe'en, for that's when the devil pees on them. For all the North American readers, an interesting fact: the blackberry was crossbred with a raspberry by a certain Judge Logan, and hence the loganberry was created.

Blackberry was also used as hedging, for even if the hedge dies, the blackberry will happily grow on and alongside the dead wood, sending out new shoots that bend down to the ground to become new roots. It is a tenacious plant, so you can use it for spells that require persistence, vigour, tenacity, and abundance. It is also good for spells of protection, and you can combine it for added effect with wild rose and any other thorn for extra power. Blackberry is connected to the element of air for its free-roaming qualities.

All over Europe the young shoots and leaves of the blackberry were used as a spring tonic, drunk as a tea.

Blackberry leaves are highly astringent, so if
you should scratch yourself, you can crush a leaf
and apply it to the scratch to stop the bleeding.

The leaves were also used as a tea to treat diarrhoea, using a double helping of the leaves. They are great in jams and are combined with apples here in England to create apple and blackberry crumble (delicious).

In the autumn, if you are out hedge riding in the land, pluck a blackberry, thank it for its aid in your Craft and savour its sweetness. That is pure magic.

Mugwort
(*Artemisia vulgaris*)

Mugwort has a very long history here in England. It grows everywhere and is often a hedgerow staple. Some consider it a weed, but we hedge witches know better. The clue is in its Latin name. It is a herb of the goddess Artemis, a wild and free lady who roams the land at her will and who is her own mistress. Mugwort has been used medicinally and magically for thousands of years, and it has a special rapport with women. It is useful for menstruation, childbirth, and menopause. This goddess of the moon knows her daughters.

The flowers and leaves can be used as a tea to help with the female reproductive system. It is also a great warming tonic, stimulating the liver and aiding the digestive system. Mugwort was used to create ale before hops were grown. But perhaps this herb's most known properties are not medicinal but magical.

On the Isle of Man, mugwort still carries importance: in fact, it is the symbolic plant used in the national celebrations held on July 5 (the old St. John's Day, before the Julian calendar came into being). The plant would be collected on St. John's Eve and made into garlands worn by the people and cattle. They would process through twin fires for protection wearing these garlands, which ensured their protection for the year. Queen Elizabeth even wore her sprig of mugwort on her royal visit in 2003.

Mugwort can also be burned
as a fumigant to cleanse an area of
negative or disturbing energies.

Simply gather up a bundle and tie together with cotton thread, hang it to dry (out of sunlight), and then, when dried, light one end and waft the bundle around the home or even your own person for purification. Outdoors, burning mugwort keeps the bugs away—brilliant for summer rituals!

Mugwort is also known for being used in divination. Making a mugwort pillow and placing it under your usual pillow grants you prophetic dreams. It's thought that it was burned in temples such as at Delphi, where the Oracle would inhale the fumes and utter prophecies. Do take care when inhaling any kind of smoke, for all smoke is harmful to the lungs.

In magic, you can fumigate an area with mugwort before a working to cleanse and purify the area (ensure that you can open windows to let in fresh air straight afterwards or do this outside). You can add the herb to any spells for an extra boost from the Goddess. You can also make a garland of the flowers at midsummer and then cast it upon the fire. You may see visions afterwards in the flames or in the smoke. Mugwort is associated with the elements of fire and air for this reason, although it can also be associated with the element of earth.

Plantain
(Plantago lanceolata)

Plantain grows anywhere and everywhere. You will find it in hedgerows, along footpaths, in fields, and in your lawn. It travels well and was named "white man's footprint" from the early North American settlers, who supposedly carried over the seeds on their footwear and thus it grew wherever they had walked. In Anglo-Saxon, it was called *waybrode/waybroede*, or waybread, denoting a plant that grew by the wayside, as well as the seeds, which can be ground and mixed with flour to make bread.[50] The young, tender leaves can be used in salads and have a nice tangy flavour.

> *Plantain is a hardy and prolific herb that*
> *is extremely beneficial to the hedge witch*
> *both medicinally and magically.*

Plantain is a great anti-inflammatory and antihistamine. The whole of the plant is useful: leaves, flowers, seeds, and root. Insect bites and stings can all be treated with this plant: simply chew up a leaf and then place it gently on the site like a poultice. It is also brilliant for treating hayfever, and when combined with nettles in a tea or tincture can help those who suffer from seasonal allergies. It can also help with hot, tired feet; keeping a fresh leaf in each shoe can give some relief on a long trek.

We have an actual recorded case of an accused witch, Bessie Smith from Scotland, using plantain. She was said to have treated "heart fevers," using a charm that is repeated over nine mornings using the "wayburn leaves."[51] Plantain is used to treat heartburn, so a heart fever is likely the same thing.

---

50 Bruton-Seal, *Hedgerow Medicine*, 127, 129.
51 Bruton-Seal, *Hedgerow Medicine*, 129.

Other spells in which plantain can lend its energy would be for persistence, perseverance, and stamina, as well as for achieving a balance in whatever situation arises. It is associated with the element of air.

Elder
(*Sambucus nigra*)

The name of the tree is thought to come from the Anglo-Saxon word *aeld*, which means "fire," curiously enough. This could be from the hollow stems, which may have been used to blow onto fires to stoke them.[52] It could also come from the Danish *Hylde Moer*, the "elder mother" or "hidden mother" (mother of the Fair Folk). Elder is also connected to the Germanic Frau Holle. This is most certainly a tree of the Goddess, if nothing else. Like the hawthorn, it is unlucky to bring its flowers into the home.

The elder is quite nondescript until it flowers or the berries are visible. Then it comes out into full glory in clouds of white blossoms or heavy with deep purple, almost black berries. In this we can see a goddess of the light half of the year as well as a goddess of the dark half of the year. But the elder is also related to the masculine: hang out under the blossoms on midsummer night, and you could be swept away by the king of the fairies. (This author keeps trying in the hopes that a certain goblin king in the form of David Bowie appears, but has yet to succeed in her endeavours.) It was said that witches had the ability to turn themselves into elder trees to escape detection.

It is quite possibly the most medicinal plant of the hedgerow, lying right there in plain sight. The blossom helps reduce a fever by increasing perspiration, much like yarrow does when brewed as a tea. It's great for colds as well, especially when used in conjunction with plantain and nettle to ease congestion and clear a blocked or runny nose. When the elder blooms, it is usually high pollen season, and anyone with allergies or asthma has to take special care. The flowers can also be distilled and then the liquid applied to

---

52 Woodland Trust, "Elder."

sunburn, cooling and soothing the skin and reducing inflammation. Elderflower cordial can also help with menopausal hot flushes.

Most people know of elderberries helping in coughs and colds, found in tincture and syrup form. You can also use them to help calm nerve inflammation, such as in migraines or sciatica. You can use the leaves to ease bruises and sprains by making it into an ointment with olive oil and beeswax. And you can just drink elderberry wine because it is delicious. Once again, strain all the seeds though because, well, cyanide!

Magically speaking, you can make incense blends with the flowers, leaves, and berries to work with the Fair Folk. You can also make spring blends with just the blossoms and autumn blends with the berries for the sabbats. You can use elder in spells of healing or when invoking the Goddess. I don't recommend tools made of the wood, such as wands or stangs/staffs of elder, unless you have specifically asked and obtained permission from the tree itself. It's too easy to mistake our own desire for something and think we have permission when we most certainly do not. Listen very closely and carefully if you do choose to do so. Always leave an offering for whatever you take, be it blossom, leaf, berry, or wood. Elder is associated with the elements of fire and earth.

• • •

This is but a short list of nine herbs that can be found in the hedgerow. I could write a whole book on just hedgerow herbs alone! For more information, please see the bibliography for some great herbal resources.

*D*elicately she picks the dark purple fruit of the blackberry. Monarch butterflies rest on nearby leaves, their wings slowly opening and closing in the heat of the autumn sun. Having grasped her prize, she brings the small fruit up to her nose and sniffs in the scent of the season. What was once a beautiful little flower is now a vibrant berry filled with the seeds of potential. It is a small rite for the hedge witch, that which heralds the beginning of the season for her: the first blackberry. She brings it to her lips and in her mind says a quiet prayer to the Goddess and God, the Fair Folk, and most especially to the spirit of the bramble, thanking it for its gift. She puts it into her mouth and the berry bursts on her tongue, the juices awakening her spirit and singing to her soul.

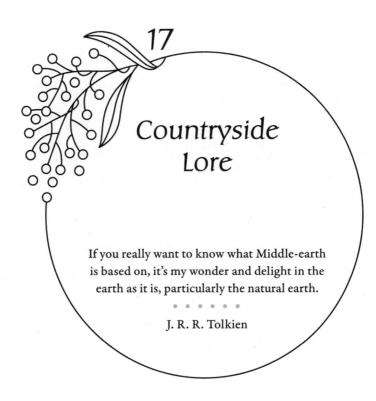

17

Countryside Lore

If you really want to know what Middle-earth
is based on, it's my wonder and delight in the
earth as it is, particularly the natural earth.

. . . . . .

J. R. R. Tolkien

The natural countryside calls to every hedge witch. Understanding how the land works, how the seasons flow, and the ways of the cycle are paramount to this aspect of the Craft. In this chapter we'll look at some of the ways that you can connect to nature and introduce you to some of the countryside lore.

Weather

Perhaps the most important thing to our rural ancestors was the weather. As such, there is a vast amount of knowledge and lore that pertains to the weather. Much of the older sayings do come from Britain but have travelled across the Atlantic to become part of the culture and colloquialisms there as well. A good witch would be able to predict the weather and so would have to notice the indicators that are around them.

Clouds

It's good to know your cirrus clouds from your cumulus and your nimbus from your stratus. Each of these can be indicators of weather that is to come. Briefly, let's look at them here. I do encourage you to delve deeper into the science of clouds to understand more. All clouds can combine together to form different shapes that help tell us what is happening in the atmosphere.

CIRRUS: These are high-altitude clouds that are seen in fair weather. They are white and very wispy.

CUMULUS: Lower down, around mid-level of the sky, you will find these clouds. These are the tall, puffy, fluffy tower-shaped clouds that are white or sometimes darkened at the bottom, sometimes grey.

NIMBUS: These are the rain clouds.

STRATUS: Like the name suggests, these are layered or striated clouds.

You can get any variation of these clouds. Fair weather is usually assured with cirrus, cumulus, cirrocumulus, and cirrostratus. Chance of rain occurs with altocumulus, nimbostratus, and stratocumulus. It will pretty much mean rain, sometimes heavy, if you spot nimbus, altostratus, nimbostratus, stratus, and cumulonimbus clouds.

Animals

Various types of animals exhibit different behaviour according to the weather. Spiders spin their webs on fine days. Bees suddenly leaving the garden in the middle of the day means rain is shortly on the way. Ants too take shelter before a storm, as do all insects. If you see lots of wasps, this usually means lots of warm, sunny weather. Butterflies too enjoy fine weather, so seeing them in large quantities usually indicates fine warm weather. Swallows, swifts, and house martins flying high in the sky indicate high pressure, while lower pressure brings the insects that they hunt closer to the ground. And, of course, we cannot forget the world-famous Punxsutawney Phil, the groundhog who lets those in the United States know whether winter is over or not, and also his lesser-known Canadian cousin, Wiarton Willie.

Old Sayings

We also have an established lore of sayings for different types of weather based on different phenomena, some of which is based on scientific fact, others perhaps on observations at that point in time relevant to a much more local pattern but that have spread out across the world.

- Red sky at night, shepherd's (or "sailor's" in North America) delight. Red sky in the morning, shepherds (or sailors) take warning.

- Ring around the moon, rain coming soon.

- Flies will swarm before a storm.

- When smoke descends (from chimneys) good weather ends. (Smoke that rises directly up into the air indicates high pressure and usually good weather. Smoke that falls downwards indicates low pressure and generally inclement weather.)

- Frogs will call before the rain but in the sun are quiet again.

- If March comes in like a lion, then it goes out like a lamb.

- If April blows its horn, it brings forth hay and also corn.

There are also sayings linked to the old sabbats but given their Christian feast names instead:

- If Candlemas (Imbolc) be fair and bright, winter will have a fight. If Candlemas brings cloud and rain, winter will not come again.

- St. Swithin's Day (around Lammas time) if it does rain, for forty days it will remain. St. Swithin's Day if it be fair, for forty days it will rain no more.

- If ducks do slide at Hallowtide (Samhain), at Christmas they will swim. If ducks do swim at Hallowtide, at Christmas they will slide. (I think this relates to bodies of water freezing over.)

- If St. Bartholomew's (Mabon) be clear, a prosperous autumn comes that year.

- Wind in the northwest on St. Martin's Day (old Samhain date pre-Julian calendar), there's a bad winter on the way. Wind in the southwest on St. Martin's Day, a mild winter and there it'll stay.

- If the sun shines through the apple branches on Christmas day, in autumn there will be a bountiful display.

Star Lore

It is also important for the hedge witch to understand something of the night sky. If nothing else, on a cloudless night you can use it to navigate as long as you can find the right star. Certain constellations also indicate the change of season, from winter to summer.

Finding North (Polaris)

If you want to know which direction is north, you must look for Polaris, the North Star. To do this, it is helpful first to find two constellations: Ursa Major and Cassiopeia. Ursa Major most people know by the seven stars that form the Plough, or the Big Dipper. On the edge of the Big Dipper's cup, farthest away from the handle, you will find that the lip leads or points to Polaris. Sometimes Ursa Major is too low in the sky to see clearly, so we can look to Cassiopeia instead, easily recognisable by its W shape formed by five stars. You don't have to worry about not finding Cassiopeia in the northern hemisphere, for it is always visible. The top left-hand star points to Polaris.

The star Polaris is part of a constellation in itself, the Little Dipper, or Ursa Minor. Polaris is right at the tip of the handle, so it's fairly easy to double check that you've got the right star from these indicators. Once you've found Polaris, face it so that Ursa Major is on your left and Cassiopeia on your right. Then you are facing north, west is left, east is right, and south is behind you.

The Hunter and the Herdsman

Two constellations presage the seasons of summer and winter in the northern hemisphere. These are Orion (the Hunter) and Boötes (the Herdsman). Winter comes with the rising of the Hunter and summer with the rising of the Herdsman. The Hunter is most visible from around Yule to the spring equinox, and the Herdsman from around Beltane to Mabon.

Easily Identifiable Stars

Other notable stars to look out for and identify are Aldebaran, a bright red star, and Sirius, or the Dog Star, the brightest star in the northern hemisphere (it's actually made up of two stars, Sirius A and Sirius B, which is why it appears so bright). The Pleiades is also a constellation to look out for, otherwise known as the Seven Sisters. It's seen in the winter tides, and its likeness has been found on a Bronze Age artefact known as the Nebra Sky Disk going back to 1600 BCE. The rising of the Pleiades heralded the new year, or at least the new agricultural year.

If you are lucky enough to live in the countryside, where there is no light pollution, you can see the band of our galaxy, the Milky Way. This is truly an awesome sight that makes you realise just how vast the worlds really are and through which you can feel how connected everything is on a grand scale.

Taking Note of Your Local Area

The hedge witch will spend much of their time outdoors noticing what is happening in the local landscape. In doing so, they will better understand the cardinal directions wherever they may find themselves, simply by being able to look at the landscape and find the indicators that point to the different directions. They will be able to tell which animals are in a certain area, even if said animals aren't to be seen, by footprints, droppings, feeding signs, scratches, clawmarks, sleeping places, and other markers of their presence.

For example, I know that the deer like to sleep in my garden, as the ornamental grasses around the pond are flattened after they have made them their beds. I also see them regularly with my own two eyes, but that's beside the point. I can tell where they've fed or munched on bushes and flowers and left droppings. I've also found owl pellets beneath the trees and on the patio. I've seen badger prints in the dirt pushed up on molehills. I can follow the tracks of the fallow deer on the heath and know by the shape of them how old the tracks are and whether the deer are close by. When coming across the hole of an underground entrance, I can tell by the shape of the hole whether it is a badger sett, a fox earth/den, or a rabbit warren.

The flora and fauna can also teach us a lot. For instance, moss tends to grow on the more northern sides of trees and rocks. Trees and bushes that are loaded with berries in the autumn tend to mean a hard winter is ahead. Oak and ash trees can help us determine if it's going to be a nice summer by when they come into leaf:

Ash before oak, we're in for a soak.
Oak before ash, we're in for a splash.

I'm also very much interested in the man-made history and archaeology of my locality. I have ordinance survey maps that tell me much about where I live. They indicate the known ancient burial sites, springs, wells, and other places of interest. Trawling through academic documents online helps me find the more obscure papers written on the five-mile radius of my village, which has Celtic and Anglo-Saxon history in the form of henges and tumuli, as well as ancient settlements that have now been destroyed by the farmer's plough. I can find ancient hedgerows and ditches and look into their history; often you can find out some really interesting information on the landowners going back hundreds of years. Names of fields can indicate what used to grow there, such as an ancient tree that was "unlucky" to cut down like the holly or the hawthorn.

It's also good to understand the local weather patterns. Where I live we have a bit of a "bubble," a microclimate that keeps our area different from areas just five miles down the road. It's important to understand this in order to grow the right things in the garden. It's equally important to understand the weather patterns and know which winds bring rain or cold weather and which ones bring favourable weather.

. . .

There are so many ways that you can connect more deeply with your local landscape using the knowledge gleaned from the countryside. Let the land speak to you; look up its history in the local library and online, and ask around with the locals. Find out where your water comes from: is it a local reservoir, river, lake, well, or borehole deep underground? Where does your food come from? Can you visit local farms or talk to local producers at farmer's markets? What can you grow on your own land, if you have any? Are there any local beekeepers near you where you can buy local honey to support them? What can you do to attract more wildlife into the garden? Are there places in your area that you can "rewild" to encourage more diversity in the wildlife, whether it is a village green or a city park? These are all suggestions to help you begin to connect on a real experiential level with your local landscape and thereby increase your connection to it. You will learn so much from it. You will deepen your knowledge and your understanding, as well as your Craft, in doing so.

*T*he rain washed the path clean of all tracks apart from those of several fallow deer. In the wet sand she could see the prints clearly, sharply outlined and very fresh. They were nearby. She knew their haunts and made her way to a patch of pine trees to see if she could spot them lurking in the shadows. Sure enough, there they were, taking a respite from the weather. They came to the trees' edge and stood looking at her with those large inquisitive eyes. She smiled and waved at them. They knew that she did not have a dog who would chase them. They didn't run from her as much as from others who may be on the heath; there was a growing trust between them. She counted the number in the herd and saw that it was thinning out in numbers, which happens in the late spring as some members leave, such as the new stags or the "teenagers" together in their little gangs, only to regroup again in the autumn. In the winter the herd was sometimes over seventy in number; it was a wonderful sight to behold. Come summer, the deer would be even harder to spot, with the bracken growing up to waist height and hiding them behind the green foliage. But for now she nodded her head, wished them well, and continued on her walk to see what else was new in the land.

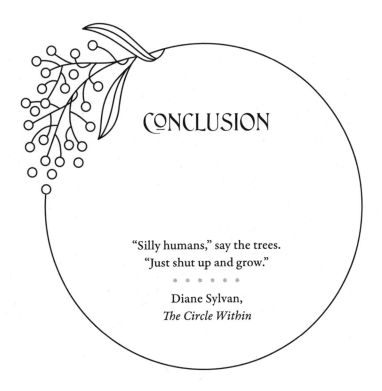

CONCLUSION

"Silly humans," say the trees.
"Just shut up and grow."

. . . . . .

Diane Sylvan,
The Circle Within

Hedge Witchcraft teaches us about ourselves through the wonders of the natural world. It tells us to listen to the wind, feel the hum of earth energy, dance around the fire, and immerse ourselves in the waters. We are so blessed to be able to commune directly with the divine and know that they are within us as much as they are in the world around us. We can change our lives through our knowledge and wisdom, be it in spellcraft, herbcraft, country lore, or any number of different crafts we might specialise in. And above all, we know that we can walk between the worlds, beneath the sun and moon and into worlds most people have never even dreamt of in their day-to-day existence.

The Old Ways may speak to you; they may sing in your soul. As such, you may choose to dedicate yourself to your path. You may decide that you want to dedicate yourself and your work to the Goddess and God or to a named deity. You have the knowledge and the resources here in this book to devise a self-dedication ritual, should you so desire. It will be an extremely personal ritual that is between you and the Goddess and God or between you and your environment alone. You will know when the time is right, as you not only feel the call of the Old Ways, but you actually live them in each and every moment.

This path is not just for the sabbats and esbats alone. The path of the hedge witch is one that is lived each day in all the small things we do, in the minutiae of life. How we operate, how we work in the world, how we interact with all things says more about our path than we could ever express with words. Our traditions cannot just be thought about; they must be put into action in order to have any effectiveness.

Our study is self-directed, and we know that we require the discipline necessary to stay the course. And we also know that we have the Goddess and the God right there beside us, as well as all the other folk that we work with, including the Fair Folk, our fylgja, and more. While we only have ourselves to be held accountable, we will want to do our best for them as well. Even if we have only glimpsed the beauty and wonder that nature holds all around us, we will want to work with it deeper, to connect and reconnect ourselves to this place in time, to find how we can fit in and be a contributing member with love and respect in our hearts.

Your tradition will become your life; it's not a hobby. You will have good days and bad days, times when your world may seem to be falling apart. But know that if you have set yourself a good foundation to work from, you will be held until you are able to come to terms with whatever life throws at you, whether it is grief, loss, despair, loneliness, or betrayal. You have worked with the elements; you know how they flow through your life and how they can inspire you and keep you going even through the roughest times. And you will have the most wonderful memories of that true, deep connection, which you can always reach out to again and again. If you know how you fit in the world even as it is falling apart around you,

you will know how to get through, one day at a time, with the Goddess and the God nearby, watching from the leafy greens of the forest glade.

The wonder of rituals held under a full moon on a beach by the sea or holding a sabbat under the light of the summer sun will shine in your heart like a beacon that keeps you from smashing against the rocks like a ship gone astray. You will know yourself better, and in knowing yourself better, you will understand others, both human and other than human. The enchantment will fill your heart with a golden glow that you can feel and which others around you may notice. Your self-belief and confidence will grow as you do the work, gaining as much knowledge from the successes as from the failures, for there are no failures, only lessons to be learned. You will be more at ease with yourself, for in loving the Goddess and the God there is no way that you cannot love yourself, too.

We all have different abilities, and we have the tools that we need to awaken our own powers. Common sense and patience, as well as determination and discernment, are our greatest tools. You will learn to trust your intuition more, for your work between the worlds has allowed you to see beyond the veil of this world and into the otherworld. You will understand how the world works because you have paid attention. You will understand how your mind works because you have paid attention.

Even as I write these words, the hawks are calling overhead. Through the open windows allowing the fresh summer breeze in after a storm, I know that they are riding the winds above me and that I can reach out to them to learn about freedom and ecstasy. In their cry is also the cry of my own heart, wild and free. May it also be so in your heart.

Bibliography

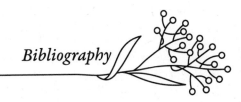

Auset, Brandi. *The Goddess Guide: Exploring the Attributes and Correspondences of the Divine Feminine*. Llewellyn, 2009.

Baker, Melinda M. "Samuel Parris: Minister at Salem Village," Scholar Works University of Indiana, https://scholarworks.iupui.edu/bitstream/handle/1805/4601/Melinda%20Baker%20-%20Samuel%20Parris%20Minister%20at%20Salem%20Village%20 3.26.14.pdf?sequence=1 (accessed 16 November 2021).

Bede, Venerabilis. *Bede: The Reckoning of Time*. Translated by Faith Wallis. Liverpool University Press, 1999.

Beth, Rae. *The Green Hedge Witch*. Hale, 2008.

———. *Spellcraft for Hedge Witches: A Guide to Healing Our Lives*. Hale, 2004.

———. *The Hedge Witch's Way: Magical Spirituality for the Lone Spellcaster*. Hale, 2001.

Bourke, Angela. *The Burning of Bridget Cleary: A True Story*. Random House, 2010.

Brigham Young University. "The Life and Legacy of the King James Bible." https://exhibits.lib.byu.edu/kingjamesbible/translating-kjb .html (accessed 16 November 2021).

Bruton-Seal, Julie, and Matthew Seal. *Hedgerow Medicine: Harvest and Make Your Own Herbal Remedies.* Merlin Unwin, 2008.

———. *The Herbalist's Bible: John Parkinson's Lost Classic Rediscovered.* Merlin Unwin, 2014.

Campanelli, Pauline. *Ancient Ways: Reclaiming Pagan Traditions.* Llewellyn, 2014.

Carr-Gomm, Philip. "Druid Wisdom." https://philipcarr-gomm.com /essay/druid-wisdom/ (accessed 1 December 2021).

———. *The Origin of Wicca and Druidry: Adapted from Druid Mysteries.* Rider, 2002. https://www.druidry.org/druid-way /other-paths/wicca-druidcraft/origins-wicca-druidry (accessed 5 July 2018).

Cater, Karen. *The Shortest Day: A Little Book of the Winter Solstice.* Hedingham Fair, 2014.

Chamberlain, Lisa. *A Wiccan's Guide and Grimoire for Working Magic with Lunar Energies.* Create Space, 2016.

———. *Wicca Herbal Magic: A Beginner's Guide to Herbal Spellcraft.* Sterling Ethos, 2021.

Crowley, Aleister. *Liber Al vel Legis (The Book of the Law).* Red Wheel Weiser, 2004.

Crowley, Vivianne. *Way of Wicca.* Thorsons, 2001.

———. *Wicca: The Old Religion in the New Millenium.* Thorsons, 1996.

Cuhulain, Kerr. *Full Contact Magick: A Book of Shadows for the Wiccan Warrior*. Llewellyn, 2002.

———. *Wiccan Warrior: Walking a Spiritual Path in a Sometimes Hostile World*. Llewellyn, 2000.

Cunningham, Scott. *The Complete Book of Incense, Oils and Brews*. Llewellyn, 2002.

———. *Earth, Air, Fire & Water: More Techniques of Natural Magic*. Llewellyn, 1993.

———. *Earth Power: Techniques of Natural Magic*. Llewellyn, 1993.

———. *Living Wicca: A Further Guide for the Solitary Practitioner*. Llewellyn, 1993.

———. *Magical Herbalism: The Secret Craft of the Wise*. Llewellyn, 2001.

———. *Wicca: A Guide for the Solitary Practitioner*. Llewellyn, 1991.

Daimler, Morgan. *Fairy Witchcraft: A Neopagan's Guide to the Celtic Fairy Faith*. Moon Books, 2014.

de Givry, Grillot. *Witchcraft, Magic and Alchemy*. Frederick Publications, 1954.

Dugan, Ellen. *Natural Witchery: Intuitive, Personal and Practical Magick*. Llewellyn, 2007.

———. *Seasons of Witchery: Celebrating the Sabbats with the Garden Witch*. Llewellyn, 2012.

Encyclopaedia Britannica. "Diana: Roman Religion." https://www.britannica.com/topic/Diana-Roman-religion (accessed 1 December 2021).

Evert Hopman, Ellen. *The Sacred Herbs of Spring: Magical, Healing and Edible Plants to Celebrate Beltaine*. Destiny Books, 2020.

Ewart Evans, George. *Ask the Fellow Who Cuts the Hay*. Faber & Faber, 2018.

———. *The Pattern Under the Plough*. Faber & Faber, 1966.

Farrar, Janet, et al. *The Healing Craft: Healing Practices for Witches and Pagans*. Phoenix, 1999.

———. *The Inner Mysteries: Progressive Witchcraft and Connection with the Divine*. Acorn Guild Press, 2012.

———. *Spells and How They Work*. Hale, 2010.

———. *Witch's Bible: The Complete Witches' Handbook*. Hale, 1984.

Fisher, Amber. *Philosophy of Wicca*. ECW Press, 2002.

Forest, Danu. *Celtic Tree Magic: Ogham Lore and Druid Mysteries*. Llewellyn, 2014.

———. *The Magical Year: Seasonal Celebrations to Honour Nature's Ever-Turning Wheel*. Watkins, 2016.

———. *Wild Magic: Celtic Folk Traditions for the Solitary Practitioner*. Llewellyn, 2020.

Franklin, Anna. *The Hearth Witch's Compendium: Magical and Natural Living for Every Day*. Llewellyn, 2017.

Franklin, Anna, and Paul Mason. *Fairy Lore*. Capall Bann, 1999.

Frazer, Sir James George. *The Golden Bough: A Study in Magic and Religion*, volume 6. Macmillan, 2009.

Freeman, Mara. *Kindling the Celtic Spirit*. HarperCollins, 2001.

Goodare, Julian. "A Royal Obsession with Black Magic Started Europe's Most Brutal Witch Hunts," *National Geographic*, https://www.nationalgeographic.co.uk/history-and-civilisation /2019/10/royal-obsession-black-magic-started-europes-most -brutal-witch (accessed 16 November 2021).

Gooley, Tristan. *The Natural Navigator: Pocket Guide.* Virgin Books, 2011.

———. *Wild Signs and Star Paths: 52 Keys That Will Open Your Eyes, Ears and Mind to the World Around You.* Sceptre, 2018.

Graves, Robert. *The White Goddess: A Historical Grammar of Poetic Myth.* Octagon, 1978.

Green, Marian. *The Gentle Arts of Natural Magic.* Thoth, 1997.

———. *Natural Witchcraft: The Timeless Arts and Crafts of the Country Witch.* Thorsons, 2001.

———. *Wild Witchcraft: A Guide to Natural, Herbal and Earth Magic.* Thorsons, 2002.

———. *A Witch Alone: Thirteen Moons to Master Natural Magic.* Thorsons, 1995.

Harte, Jeremy. *Explore Fairy Traditions.* Heart of Albion Press, 2004.

Heselton, Philip. *Doreen Valiente: Witch.* Centre for Pagan Studies, 2016.

Howard, Michael. *East Anglian Witches and Wizards.* Three Hands Press, 2017.

———. *Modern Wicca: A History from Gerald Gardner to the Present.* Llewellyn, 2010.

Hughes, Kristoffer. *Natural Druidry.* Thoth, 2007.

Hutton, Ronald. *Stations of the Sun: A History of the Ritual Year in Britain.* Oxford University Press, 2001.

———. *The Triumph of the Moon: A History of Modern Pagan Witchcraft.* Oxford University Press, 2001.

———. *The Witch: A History of Fear, from Ancient Times to the Present.* Yale University Press, 2018.

Jenner, Paul, et al. *The Outdoor Pocket Bible.* Crimson, 2008.

K, Amber, and Azrael Arynn K. *How to Become a Witch: The Path of Nature, Spirit & Magic*. Llewellyn, 2010.

Kelden. *The Crooked Path: An Introduction to Traditional Witchcraft*. Llewellyn, 2020.

Kelly, Aidan. "About Naming Ostara, Litha, and Mabon." www .patheos.com/blogs/aidankelly/2017/05/naming-ostara-litha -mabon (accessed 2 December 2021).

Kirk, Robert. *The Secret Commonwealth of Elves, Fauns and Fairies*. New York Review Books Classics, 2007.

Krappe, Alexander H. "Old Celtic Taboos." *Folklore* 53, no. 4 (1942): 196–208. http://www.jstor.org/stable/1257371.

Kynes, Sandra. *Star Magic: The Wisdom of the Constellations for Pagans and Wiccans*. Llewellyn, 2015.

Lipp, Deborah. *The Way of Four Spellbook: Working Magic with the Elements*. Llewellyn, 2006.

Mankey, Jason. *Transformative Witchcraft: The Greater Mysteries*. Llewellyn, 2019.

Mather, Cotton. *Wonders of the Invisible World*. Devoted Publishing, 2017.

Matthews, Caitlín. *The Elements of the Celtic Tradition*. Element Books, 1989.

McGarry, Gina. *Brighid's Healing: Ireland's Celtic Medicine Traditions*. Green Magic, 2007.

Murphy-Hiscock, Arin. *Solitary Wicca for Life: A Complete Guide to Mastering the Craft on Your Own*. Provenance Press, 2005.

———. *The Green Witch: Your Complete Guide to the Natural Magic of Herbs, Flowers, Essential Oils and More*. Adams Media, 2017.

Parker, Will. *The Four Branches of the Mabinogi*. Bardic Press, 2007.

Paxson, Diana L. "The Return of the Völva," *Seeing for the People.* https://seidh.org/articles/seidh (accessed 1 December 2021).

Pearson, Nigel. *The Devil's Plantation: East Anglian Lore, Witchcraft & Folk Magic.* Troy Books, 2016.

———. *Walking the Tides: Seasonal Rhythms and Traditional Lore in Natural Craft.* Capall Bann, 2009.

Penczak, Christopher. *The Inner Temple of Witchcraft: Magick, Meditation and Psychic Development.* Llewellyn, 2002.

Pennick, Nigel. *Runic Lore and Legend: Wyrdstaves of Old Northumbria.* Destiny Books, 2019.

Purcell, Clíona. "Waterford Treasures: The Blog." https://waterfordtreasures.wixsite.com/wattreasuresblog/post /the-burning-of-bridget-cleary-witches-fairies-and-the-danger-of -superstition (accessed 6 December 2021).

Saille, Harmonia. *Hedge Riding.* Moon Books, 2012.

Sanderson, Stewart. "A Prospect of Fairyland." *Folklore* 75, spring 1964: 1–18. https://www.jstor.org/stable/1258872?seq=1.

Sheppard, Susan. *A Witch's Runes.* Citadel Press, 1998.

Starhawk. *The Earth Path: Grounding Your Spirit in the Rhythms of Nature.* HarperCollins, 2005.

Struthers, Jane. *Red Sky at Night: The Book of Lost Countryside Wisdom.* Ebury Press, 2009.

Tennyson, Lord Alfred. *Idylls of the King.* Robbins Digital Library Projects, University of Rochester. https://d.lib.rochester.edu /camelot/text/tennyson-idylls-of-the-king.

Thomas, Valerie. *Of Chalk and Flint: A Way of Norfolk Magic.* Troy Books, 2020.

Telyndru, Jhenah. *Avalon Within: A Sacred Journey of Myth, Mystery, and Inner Wisdom.* Llewellyn, 2010.

Tzu, Sun. *The Art of War.* T. Cleary, trans. Shambhala, 1991.

UK Parliament, "Witchcraft." https://www.parliament.uk/about /living-heritage/transformingsociety/private-lives/religion /overview/witchcraft/ (accessed 13 July 2022).

University College London. "The Names of the Moons." http://www .homepages.ucl.ac.uk/~ucapsj0/moon/index.html (accessed 1 December 2021).

Valiente, Doreen. *An ABC of Witchcraft.* Robert Hale, 1986.

van der Hoeven, Joanna. *The Book of Hedge Druidry: A Complete Guide for the Solitary Seeker.* Llewellyn, 2019.

———. *The Hedge Druid's Craft: An Introduction to Walking Between the Worlds of Wicca, Witchcraft and Druidry.* Moon Books, 2018.

Wilson, Lori Lee. *The Salem Witch Trials.* Lerner Publications, 1997.

Woodland Trust. "Elder." https://www.woodlandtrust.org.uk /trees-woods-and-wildlife/british-trees/a-z-of-british-trees/elder/ (accessed 18 January 2022).

Wright, John. *The Forager's Calendar: A Seasonal Guide to Nature's Wild Harvests.* Profile Books, 2019.

To Write to the Author
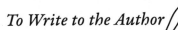

If you wish to contact the author or would like more information about this book, please write to the author in care of Llewellyn Worldwide and we will forward your request. Both the author and the publisher appreciate hearing from you and learning of your enjoyment of this book and how it has helped you. Llewellyn Worldwide cannot guarantee that every letter written to the author can be answered, but all will be forwarded. Please write to:

Joanna van der Hoeven
℅ Llewellyn Worldwide
2143 Wooddale Drive
Woodbury, MN 55125–2989
Please enclose a self-addressed stamped envelope for reply
or $1.00 to cover costs. If outside the USA, enclose
an international postal reply coupon.

• • •

Many of Llewellyn's authors have websites with additional information and resources. For more information, please visit our website:

www.llewellyn.com